Plotinus, *Tolma*, and the Descent of Being

American University Studies

Series V
Philosophy
Vol. 135

PETER LANG
New York • San Francisco • Bern • Baltimore
Frankfurt am Main • Berlin • Wien • Paris

N. Joseph Torchia

Plotinus, *Tolma*, and the Descent of Being

An Exposition and Analysis

PETER LANG
New York • San Francisco • Bern • Baltimore
Frankfurt am Main • Berlin • Wien • Paris

Library of Congress Cataloging-in-Publication Data

Torchia, N. Joseph (Natale Joseph)
  Plotinus, tolma, and the descent of being : an exposition and analysis
/ N. Joseph Torchia.
    p. cm. — (American university studies. Series V, Philosophy ;
vol. 135)
  Includes bibliographical references.
  1. Plotinus. Enneads. I. Title. II. Series.
B693.E6T67   1993   186'.4—dc20   91-35593
ISBN 0-8204-1768-8   CIP
ISSN 0739-6392

Die Deutsche Bibliothek-CIP-Einheitsaufnahme

Torchia, Natale Joseph:
Plotinus, tolma, and the descent of being : an exposition and analysis /
N. Joseph Torchia.—New York; Berlin; Bern; Frankfurt/M.; Paris;
Wien: Lang, 1993
    (American university studies : Ser. 5, Philosophy ; Vol. 135)
    ISBN 0-8204-1768-8
NE: American university studies/05

The paper in this book meets the guidelines for permanence and
durability of the Committee on Production Guidelines for
Book Longevity of the Council on Library Resources.

Table of Contents

In Memory Of My Maternal And Paternal

Grandparents

Lux perpetua luceat eis.

Introduction

In its broadest terms, this study involves an investigation of the *Enneads* of Plotinus (204-270 A.D.), the key representative of the later Greek philosophical movement known as "Neoplatonism" and a dominant influence upon the development of early Christian philosophy and theology. More specifically, I will isolate certain elements in Plotinus's writings which exhibit an apparent pessimism toward the very emergence of being. In this respect, I will address those passages in the *Enneads* which offer the reader an account of the procession of being from the One that stands in sharp contrast to Plotinus's optimistic account of the One's natural emanation and self-diffusiveness. In this alternate account (or more precisely, in these alternate *accounts*), Plotinus attributes the emergence of being to a voluntary, and hence, blameworthy will that manifests itself as an act of *tolma* or audacity for otherness from the One, or on lower ontological levels, for separation from higher intelligible reality.

The Problem Defined

My interest in this topic grew out of an investigation of the Plotinian heritage of St. Augustine of Hippo's moral theory. In assessing Augustine's intellectual dependence on Plotinus, I chiefly focused upon the affinities between their theories of the soul's fall.[1] These investigations led me to an analysis of the term *tolma* (τόλμα), the prime motive for the soul's descent in Plotinus's philosophy. In that term, I found a potential key to the pessimistic side of Plotinus alluded to above. *Tolma* has a long and rich history, assuming a prominence in Neopythagoreanism, in Middle Platonism, in the fall speculation of the Hermetic writers, and in other ancient sources. Moreover, *tolma* assumed a prominent position in the dualistic schemes of Gnosticism. Accordingly, its presence in the *Enneads* raises an important question: why did Plotinus rely upon the terminology and insights of the very sects which he so vehemently opposed? From this standpoint, I came to realize that more detailed study of the significance of Plotinian *tolma* might reveal some overlooked textures on the surface of Plotinus's thought.

Tolma remains a rather problematic component of Plotinian philosophy. At the outset of my investigations, I was struck by the fact that the term stands out as something of an anomaly in Plotinus's accounts of the descending movement of being from the One. It was my observation, however, that commentators tend to dismiss this feature of his thought as irrelevant, to relegate it to an insignificant role, or to bypass it altogether. The notable exception to this trend is Naguib Baladi's book-length treatment of the notion of audacity in the *Enneads*, *La pensée de Plotin* (Paris: Presses Universitaires de France, 1970).[2] In the present work, I will neither challenge nor attempt to supersede the substance of Baladi's competent study. But after a lapse of more than twenty years, I think that this particular area of Plotinian thought invites some renewed analysis. In this respect, my work seeks to provide another extended discussion of an intriguing and much neglected area of Plotinian studies. ·

As Baladi ably demonstrated, *tolma* assumed a key metaphysical role in Plotinus's vision of reality as a whole. My study continues in the same vein, but concentrates chiefly upon the relationship between *tolma* and what might be characterized as the "problem of otherness" in the *Enneads*. In my estimation, this problem encompasses the dual question as to *how* and *why* any reality other than the One must emerge. In this regard, it appears that a greater sensitivity to the role of *tolma* in the *Enneads* could serve to clarify the scope of Plotinus's ambivalence regarding reality other than the One. From this perspective, the negative sentiments toward lower levels of reality that we occasionally encounter in Plotinus might not be so many odd (and in some contexts, inexplicable) inconsistencies on his part, but instead, expressions of a viewpoint which permeates the *Enneads*.

This study will assess the extent of such a viewpoint in Plotinus, with a specific focus upon his use of *tolma* or closely related language. In various treatises, the substantive *tolma*, its verbal and adjectival forms, and terminology expressing the same sentiments designate a will toward separate existence—an affective movement which is instrumental in the emanation of being from the One. Because *tolma* (the primary focus of this study) has such apparent Gnostic, Hermetic, and Neopythagorean overtones, it provides an intriguing referent which can, I think, enable us to trace a pessimistic strain running throughout the Plotinian *corpus*.

The Metaphysical Dimension of Plotinian *Tolma*

An adequate understanding of the descending movement of being from the One in Plotinus's scheme necessitates a close examination of that scheme as a whole. This study will address itself to the metaphysics of Plotinus, the background against which the role of *tolma* in the descent of *Nous* and the different phases of Soul will be analyzed. Because the Plotinian metaphysics is rather complex and technical, I will address its more salient features, attempting to provide something of a broad overview of the rich terrain of the *Enneads*.

It is apparent that Plotinus's vision of reality underwent some interesting changes throughout his intellectual career. In this regard, the question of a "genetic development" will be assessed later in this study. But for the present purposes, I will proceed from the tentative assumption of stability and non-development within the *Enneads*. This will allow for something of a base upon which I will build my subsequent exposition and analysis.

The intelligible universe of Plotinus is characterized by two key movements: first, an outward emanation from an absolutely transcendent principle of unity (πρόοδος); secondly, an ascent or return of being to its source (ἐπιστροφή). This universe constitutes a hierarchical scheme composed of three levels or hypostases: the One, *Nous* or Intellect, and Soul. The process of emanation from the One is responsible for the production or generation of the lower hypostases, as well as those lesser degrees of reality which include Nature and the material cosmos. Each hypostasis provides a different manifestation of the same ontological power and life. Reality or being proceeds from a common center or nexus, like the procession of spokes from the hub of a wheel. For purposes of exposition, Plotinus himself uses the example of many lines radiating from one center to explain this movement (*Ennead* VI.5(23).5.1-10). *Nous* and Soul are dependent upon the One for their very existence and stand in a subordinate relationship to their primal cause. [3]

The procession of *Nous* and Soul has no effect whatsoever upon the One. It remains unchanged and undiminished in the process. Moreover, the One emanates in a purely spontaneous manner. Unlike the free creative activity associated with the Judeo-Christian God, the Plotinian One generates being because it must—indeed, it is its very nature to do so. Yet, it would be erroneous to view the One as determined by any external influences or even by its own nature. This seemingly paradoxical character of emanation as both spontaneous and necessary is significant, insofar as it establishes the vital relationship between the One's nature and its emanation or outpouring. Emanation is spontaneous because it involves neither forethought nor volition: it merely occurs. Emanation is necessary because the One is naturally self-diffusive and hence, must overflow in the production of lesser degrees of reality. This point underscores the Plotinian dictum that a principle of perfection must generate, communicate, or share its goodness. The One's self-diffusiveness is concomitant with the emergence of being and by implication, multiplicity. [4]

But the very generation of otherness (that is, anything other than the One) constitutes a major problem in Plotinian metaphysics. While Plotinus explicitly asserts that no otherness is present in the One, he maintains that the manifold is somehow derived from this supreme principle.[5] As already stated, the One must generate multiplicity in response to its natural self-diffusiveness. But therein lies the problem: how can a source of pure unity and simplicity generate a universe of plurality, while itself remaining unaffected? Plotinus's theory of emanation, reinforced by various metaphors, attempts to bridge the gap between the One and its effects. In spite of this, we find a pronounced monistic emphasis running throughout the *Enneads*.

Plotinus frequently extols the primal unity of the One over the differentiation of generated being. In *Ennead* V.1(10).6.6-7, he queries why the One did not remain in itself (ἀλλ᾽ οὐκ ἔμεινεν ἐκεῖνο ἐφ᾽ ἑαυτοῦ. . .), or, in MacKenna's classic rendering, "self-gathered"? The difficulty lies in the fact that if the One had remained self-contained, there could exist neither being, plurality, nor motion. If Plotinus was to avoid the Parmenidean dilemma, he had to account for the emergence of the manifold from the One. The alternative would be a frozen nexus of stability and oneness. The One itself never becomes many, but the many somehow proceeds from the One. The consequence is that anything other than the One must be less than the One in dignity and power.[6]

A final point must be made. A close examination of the *Enneads* discloses that Plotinus can be rather inconsistent or even ambiguous on a number of key issues. The tentative nature of his deliberations on various topics (e.g., the varieties of Soul, the ontological status of matter, the motive for the soul's presence to matter) must be continually borne in mind. The reader of the *Enneads* encounters certain troublesome and occasionally, unresolvable tensions. Some of these have a direct bearing upon the subject matter of this study. In a few cases, conclusions can extend only as far as the content of the *Enneads* permits. In other cases, I believe that one must be willing to go beyond what Plotinus himself says and fill in the gaps with critical judgments based upon an appreciation of the *Enneads* as an organic whole.

In my estimation, Plotinus stands as one of the most powerful metaphysicians and religious thinkers that the western intellectual tradition has produced. It is my hope that the rather narrow parameters of the present work will do at least minimal justice (or as little injustice as possible) to his rich thought. My own attempt to penetrate the profundity of the *Enneads* has enabled me to appreciate something of the import of Stephen Mackenna's contention that the translation and interpretation of Plotinus is "really worth a life."[7] Accordingly, I do not claim to offer the reader any conclusive or definitive statement on this topic. What I do try to provide is a comprehensive survey of an issue that enters into every aspect of Plotinus's metaphysics, and in my opinion, demands further exploration if we are to fully appreciate the scope and extent of the problem of otherness in that scheme.

Methodology

The substance of this study entails a delineation of the role of *tolma* in the *Enneads*. At the outset, I will provide a survey of the literary, philosophical, and theological origins of the term *tolma*. Such an historical survey opens the way for a more detailed analysis of the role of *tolma* in the Plotinian scheme, an examination of its relation to other fall motives, and an evaluation of its significance in Plotinus's thought as a whole. In carrying this out, I will address the role and operation of the three hypostases of the One, *Nous*, and Soul, and their relationship to the material cosmos. To some extent, I will also grapple with the various interpretations of Soul which have emerged, attempting to provide something of a "working hypothesis" on this topic for the purposes of my investigation. This hypothesis should add some clarity to my discussions of the genesis of Soul and the descent of individual souls.

In my concluding sections, I take a closer look at the question of a possible development of thought in the *Enneads* and the degree to which Plotinus's reaction against the Gnostics might have prompted him to reject the use of *tolma* and similar terminology. In this connection, I also consider the possible affinity between Plotinus and the Gnostic tradition, and the extent to which his use of *tolma*-language supports such a hypothesis. This assessment will take into account such factors as Plotinus's historical setting, his intellectual relationship to other thinkers, and what is perhaps most significant, the unique temperament which might well have moved him in certain philosophical directions.

A Word About Texts and Forms of Citation

All references to the original Greek text of Plotinus's *Enneads* are based upon the critical edition of Paul Henry and Hans-Rudolf Schwyzer, *Plotini Opera*, Museum Lessianum Series Philosophica (XXXIII, XXXIV, XXXV), *Tomus I, II* (Paris: Desclée De Brouwer; Bruxelles: L'Edition Universell, S.A., 1951, 1959); *Tomus III* (Bruxelles: Desclée De Brouwer; Leiden: E.J. Brill, 1973). All references to the *Enneads* are provided in standard form, e.g., *Ennead* V.1(10).1, 1-10, indicating a quotation from lines 1 through 10 of the first chapter of the Fifth *Ennead*, the tenth treatise in Porphyry's chronological ordering (designated by the number within the parentheses).

Acknowledgements

While I am indebted to many individuals on a variety of levels for their assistance in the preparation and completion of this book, I wish to express my special gratitude to my doctoral dissertation mentor for encouraging my interest in this topic some nine years ago. I also wish to thank the editor of *Augustinian Studies* for permission to reprint in *Appendix B* (in a somewhat modified form), the substance of an article which originally appeared in *Augustinian Studies XVIII* (1987): 66-80. Last but not least, I wish to extend my thanks to the staff of The Institute of Christian Oriental Research (ICOR) at The Catholic University of America in Washington, D.C., for generous advice and guidance in the use of their fine holdings in the area of Nag Hammadi studies.

Notes

1. N. Joseph Torchia, "Plotinian *Tolma* and the Fall of the Soul in the Early Philosophy of Saint Augustine," *Dissertation Abstracts International* 48, No. 4 (1987), 941A (Fordham University).

   The dissertation tested, from one particular perspective, the hypothesis that the *Enneads* of Plotinus provided the philosophical matrix within which St. Augustine of Hippo articulated a key feature of his early theory of human beings as "fallen souls." This perspective focused precisely upon Augustine's triadic understanding of primal sin or *iniquitas* and its relationship to the soul's fall. The analysis assessed the extent to which *tolma* (the term which designates the prime motive for differentiation, the initiation of temporal process, and the soul's descent into matter) provides a means of illuminating Augustine's moral triad of pride (*superbia*), curiosity (*curiositas*), and carnal concupiscence (*concupiscentia carnis*).

2. Baladi's book is further supplemented by his article "Origine et Signification de l'Audace chez Plotin," in *Le Néoplatonisme* (Royaumant, 1971), pp. 89-99. In addition to Baladi's work on the subject, several other briefer treatments should be noted. John Rist offers a detailed statement on Plotinian *tolma* in his "Monism: Plotinus and Some Predecessors," *Harvard Studies in Classical Philology* 69 (1965): 329-344. Likewise important are A.H. Armstrong's contributions, found in *The Cambridge History of Later Greek and Early Medieval Philosophy* (Cambridge: Cambridge University Press, 1970), pp. 242 ff., and in "Gnosis and Greek Philosophy" in *Gnosis*, a Festschrift für Hans Jonas (Göttingen, 1978), pp. 116 ff.

3. *Ennead* V.2(11).1.9-21; cf. *Ennead* V.1(10).6.41-48.

4. *Ennead* IV.8(6).6.1-5. A.H. Armstrong (*Plotinus: A Volume of Selections*, London, 1953, p. 33) provides what John M. Rist describes as "perhaps the best traditional account of the way emanation takes place" (*Plotinus: The Road to Reality*, Cambridge, 1967, p. 67). Armstrong's definition runs as follows: "*Nous* proceeds from the One and Soul from *Nous* without in any way affecting its Source. There is no activity on the part of the One, still less any willing or planning or choice. There is simply a giving out which leaves the Source unchanged and undiminished. But though this giving out is necessary, in the sense that it cannot be conceived as not happening otherwise, it is also entirely spontaneous: There is no room

for any sort of binding or constraint, internal or external, in Plotinus's thought about the One."

5. *Ennead* V.1(10).6.16-19. cf. *Ennead* III.8(30).10.14-19.

6. *Ennead* V.1(10).6.37-45. cf. *Ennead* VI.7(38).8.17-22; *Enneads* III.8(30). 8.31-38; V.4(7).l.1-13; V.3(49).l5.7-11. The One is naturally self-diffusive but undergoes neither diminution nor dissipation by virtue of its outpouring. There exists what E. R. Dodds ("Tradition and Personal Achievement in the Philosophy of Plotinus," in *The Ancient Concept of Progress* (Oxford, 1973), p. 131) described as a "non-reciprocating" relationship between the One and its effects: ". . . the higher determines the lower without itself being determined or modified by its own causative activity . . ."

7. E.R. Dodds, editor. *Journal and Letters of Stephen Mackenna* (New York: William Morrow and Company, 1937), p. 117 (for journal entry of January 15, 1908).

Chapter I

The Sources of Plotinian *Tolma*:
An Historical Survey

Tolma is an extremely fertile term, possessing a variety of meanings. In a philosophical context, its roots are directly traceable to a number of Hellenic and Hellenistic sources. This is an important consideration when one examines its role in the *Enneads*. In various Plotinian treatises, *tolma*, its variant forms, and language conveying the same ideas express the idea of a dynamic will toward separate existence, an affective movement which is instrumental in the emanation of being from the One.[1] In each of these instances, *tolma*-language is bound-up with the notions of differentiation and otherness. Existence itself, the direct result of the One's outflow, is somehow dependent upon a desire for independence and autonomy. In this respect, the separation of *Nous* or Intellect from the One and the dispersion of Soul from the self-contained life of *Nous* constitute illegitimate acts of self-assertion.[2]

In *tolma* we find a plethora of connotations.[3] The very complexity of meaning inherent in the term, and the cluster of ideas associated with it, demands a thoroughgoing analysis of its origins and use within the Greek tradition. Accordingly, this survey will examine *tolma*'s role in the classical authors, in Neopythagorean and Middle Platonic philosophy, in the Alexandrian tradition, in the Hermetic literature, and in Gnosticism. Such a survey should provide a firmer basis upon which to conduct an investigation of the meaning of *tolma*-language in the *Enneads*.

Tolma in Classical Greek Authors

The substantive *tolma* and its variants appear in a number of sources drawn from the classical tradition: the Homeric writings, the early poets, the tragedies of Euripides, Sophocles, and Aeschylus, and to a limited extent, in Plato's philosophy. In its initial appearances, *tolma* (or related language) expressed a rather positive element in human nature. The literature of this period reflects a general preoccupation with questions concerning fate, and the problem of evil, coupled with a distrust of nature and the gods. Such attitudes fostered an emphasis upon forebearance before insurmountable obstacles and a kind of stoical acceptance of misfortune.[4] The themes of endurance, resignation to one's fate, and courageous daring are all prominent in the early writings.

In Homer"s *Iliad* and *Odyssey*, the verb *tolmao* (τολμέω) connotes a courageousness in undertaking difficult tasks or a "taking heart" in the commission of heroic deeds.[5] In the poets, one finds the widespread conviction that humans are little more than pawns in the hands of powers and forces beyond their control. This is consistent with the pessimistic religious belief that the gods hold humanity in continual check, preventing people from rising above their mortal station. In this context, the only alternative was to accept the inexorable decrees of Fate and Destiny.[6] Theognis, for one, counselled his readers to "bear up . . . in ill fortune," enduring that which the gods mete out to mortals and patiently tolerating one's lot. [7]

In classical Greek tragedy, tolma expressed an audacity or brazenness in the face of divine authority. Any attempt to overstep one's bounds's constituted a sacrilegious act of impiety. The application of *tolma*-language in this manner is prominent in Aeschylus's *Prometheus*, where the protagonist exhibits a blend of reckless courage and a bold defiance of divine commands.[8] It is interesting to observe that at this point, *tolma* assumed a decidedly pejorative connotation, expressing a renegade spirit which pits the individual against either the gods or the human community at large. One finds this connotation in subsequent philosophical and theological usages of the term.

In Plato's dialogues, we see what is apparently the first application of *tolma*-language in a philosophical context. As used by

Plato, this terminology suggests the audaciousness of a new philosophical movement which challenges more traditional teachings. In a significant passage in the *Sophist*, Plato has the "Stranger" articulate something all but anathema in the Eleatic tradition—he speaks of "that which is not."

> Wheareas we have not merely shown that things that are not are, but we have brought to light the real character of 'not-being.' We have shown that the nature of the different has existence and is parceled out over the field of existent things with reference to one another, and of every part of it that is set in contrast to 'that which is' we have dared to say that precisely that is really 'that which is not (ἐτολμήσαμεν εἰπειν ὡς αὐτὸ τοῦτό ἐστιν ὄντως τὸ μη ὄν). 9

When Plato refutes Parmenidean doctrine, he relies upon the verb "ετολμήσαμεν," which expresses a kind of daring or audacity. In effect, Plato challenges a central Eleatic teaching: by even referring to "that which is not," one ascribes some sort of ontological status to the non-existent. But how can one meaningfully speak about that which is not? Plato's assertion that the negation of difference is not the same as absolute non-being requires a certain amount of daring, precisely because it goes against the grain of an established philosophical tradition.

In the *Theaetetus*, the verb τολμήσω appears in an passage in which Socrates proposes to define the meaning of knowledge. But this might constitute an impropriety, since Socrates has already purported *not* to *know* what it means to know.

> *Theaetetus*: Well, but how are you going to carry on a discussion, Socrates, if you keep clear of those words?
> *Socrates*: I cannot, being the man I am, though I might if I were an expert in debate. If such a person were here now, he would profess to keep clear of them and rebuke us severely for my use of language. As we are such bunglers, then, shall I be so bold as to describe what knowing is like (βούλει τολμήσω εἰπεῖν οἷόν εστι τὸ επιστασθαι)? 10

In Platonic terms, the intelligible discussion of something demands a knowledge of its nature or essence. The very attempt to discuss knowledge in the absence of true knowledge constitutes a rather bold act which the verb τολμήσω expresses. Socrates wishes to avoid the presumptuousness of claiming to know what *he does not know*. Such presumptuousness characterized his Sophist opponents, those experts in the art of debate to whom he alludes. As Plato queries in the *Apology*, "Is not this ignorance of a disgraceful sort, the ignorance which is the conceit that a man knows what he does not know?"[11] Like the "Stranger" in the *Sophist*, Socrates recognizes a certain amount of daring in his assertion. In this respect, Plato's applications of *tolma*-language are consistent with what one finds in other classical Greek authors.

Tolma and the Neopythagorean Dyad

The most immediate philosophical precursors of Plotinus were the Neopythagorean thinkers of the first and second centuries A.D. Neopythagoreanism was a highly eclectic movement, representing a synthesis of Platonic, Aristotelian, and Stoic teachings coupled with an emphasis upon divine revelation, bodily discipline and numerical symbolism. It should be noted that the Neopythagorean preoccupation with number-theory was more intense than in the older Pythagorean school.[12] The Neopythagoreans, or Platonists under a Neopythagorean influence, anticipated some Plotinian teachings, including the triad of divine hypostases, the so-called "Neoplatonic Trinity." [13]

A major issue with which the Neopythagoreans grappled (as would Plotinus), concerned the perennial philosophical and religious problem of evil: how does one reconcile an essentially good godhead with a world that is characterized by imperfection and exhibits evil? The Neopythagoreans attempted to resolve this problem by means of a numerical opposition between unity and multiplicity, oddness and evenness, *Monad* and *Dyad* respectively.[14] Closely connected with the moral problem of evil was the question concerning the origin of plurality.

Neopythagorean number-theory became the basis of a thoroughgoing dualism in which the *Monad* (the principle of unity) was identified with goodness, spirit, or intelligence and the *Dyad* (the principle of multiplicity) was associated with indeterminateness and irrationality. It should be noted that scholars distinguish between two distinct schools of such theorists. This distinction is based upon evidence provided by Sextus Empiricus (*Adv. math.* X, 281ff.): one reduced everything to the opposing principles of the One and the *Dyad*, the other reduced everything to the One which engenders the *Dyad* as well as everything else.

Neopythagorean dualism must be distinguished from its more radical Gnostic and Zoroastrian counterparts. The Neopythagoreans upheld the essential goodness of the cosmos in a manner consistent with Platonism and Hellenic rationalism in general. For them, the life of the cosmos was viewed in dialectical terms as a smooth, vertical downflow of being from a divine principle that resulted in the generation of the lower world.[15] In this respect, they perceived a tension between principles of unity and plurality rather than between principles of goodness and evil as such. Nonetheless, the negative connotations associated with the *Dyad* (i.e., indeterminacy and irrationality) were, for all practical purposes, concomitant with evil.

Plato and his successors had defined the Indefinite *Dyad* in terms of deficiency and imperfection. According to Aristotle, Plato presented the One and the Indefinite *Dyad* as opposing first principles.[16]   For Plato, it appears that the *Dyad* represented that which is infinitely divisible (and infinitely large and small), while the One constituted the Principle which imposes form and limit upon the former amorphous, limitless principle.[17]   By virtue of this imposition of form and limit upon the Dyad, the One produces the numerical Ideas. [18]

Subsequent Platonists maintained this polarity between the One (or Monad) and the *Dyad*, but posited different relationships between them.[19]   For Speusippus (c. 407-339 B.C.), the Indefinite *Dyad* was the basis of multiplicity and differentiation.[20] Xenocrates (396-314 B.C.) also posited the Monad and *Dyad* as opposing first principles. But he imparted a negative character to the *Dyad*, likewise viewing it as a principle of disorder and apparently, identifying it with an evil World Soul.[21] The treatment of the *Dyad* as a principle underlying formlessness and disorder is likewise present in Plutarch of Chaeronea (45-c. 125 A.D.).[22]

In later Platonists such as Speusippus, Xenocrates, and Plutarch, then, a clear Pythagorean orientation is evident. This orientation expresses itself through their interest in the symbolism of numbers and in their delineation of the relationship between first and second Principles of the universe. In the initial centuries of the Christian era, thinkers who openly identified themselves with the Pythagorean tradition further refined the notion of the *Dyad*. It is here that we find an explicit connection between this principle and *tolma*. For the present purposes, I will confine myself to a consideration of two of these thinkers: Moderatus of Gades and Numenius of Apamea.

Moderatus's views on this topic emerge in a passage which Armstrong describes as one which "strikingly anticipates Plotinian Neoplatonism . . ."[23] He is referring to Simplicius's quote of Moderatus's teaching. Let us consider this detailed and illuminating passage in full:

> . . . in the second book of Matter Porphyry, citing from Moderatus, has also written that the Unitary Logos—as Plato somewhere says—intending to produce from himself the origin of being, by self-privation left room to quantity, depriving it of all his ratios and ideas. He called this quantity, shapeless, undifferentiated, and formless, but receptible of shape, form, differentiation, quality, etc. It is this quantity, he says, to which Plato apparently applies various predicates, speaking of the 'all-receiver', of that which is bare of species, 'the invisible' and 'the least capable of participating in the intelligible' and 'barely seizable by pseudo-reasoning' and everything similar to such predicates. This quantity (αὕτη δὲ ἡ ποσότης), he says, and this species, viz. thought of in the sense of being privation of the Unitary Logos which contains in himself all ratios of beings, are paradigms of the matter of bodies (καὶ τοῦτο τὸ εἶδος τὸ κατὰ στέρησιν τοῦ ἑνιαίου λόγου νοούμενον τοῦ πάντας τοὺς λόγους τῶν ὄντων ἐν ἑαυτῷ περιειληφότος παραδείγματά ἐστι τῆς τῶν σωμάτων ὕλης), which itself, he says, was called quantity by Pythagoreans and Plato, not in the sense of quantity as an idea, but in the sense of privation, paralysis, dispersion, and severance and because of its deviating from that which is—for which reason matter seems to be evil, as it flees that which is good. And this matter is caught by it and is not permitted to overstep its boundaries, as dispersion receives the ratio of ideal magnitude and is bounded by it, and as severance is by numerical distinction rendered eidetic. Thus, according to this exposition matter is nothing else but deviation of sensible species from intelligible ones, as the former turn away from there and are borne down towards non-being.[24]

The foregoing quote provides a clear statement regarding the separation of matter from the One: matter results from a diversion or turning away from the intelligible and a corresponding movement toward the non-being of matter. Because matter represents a deviation from that which is good, it constitutes evil (or "seems" to be such). While we find no explicit reference to the Dyad in the passage, a link between this notion and matter can be rather easily inferred. As Dillon suggests, the "quantity" (that is, *posotês*) which is discussed is none other than Indefinite *Dyad* "under another title." [25]

Similar themes are present in Numenius, whose speculative system probably represents the best anticipation of Plotinian philosophy. Porphyry, in fact (*Vita Plotini* 17), alludes to the charge that Plotinus had been accused of plagiarizing from Numenius's works. Indeed, Numenius explicitly formulated two of the central laws of Neoplatonism: *first*, the idea of participation; *secondly*, the idea of an "undiminished giving," whereby the cause is never dissipated among its effects.[26] In addition, Numenius upheld the doctrine of a divine hierarchy of three principles or hypostases: a first god, a second god or Demiurge, and a third god or World Soul. He also maintained an extreme dualism between higher and lower orders of reality, and between rational and irrational souls.[27] Numenius's pessimism toward the material order is reflected in his teaching that the soul's presence in the body results from a fall or decline.

For Numenius, matter is identified with the Indefinite *Dyad*. Like his predecessors, he maintained that the *Dyad* prompts a dispersion of some higher intelligible reality. In this context, matter splits the second god or Demiurge in two. This division proceeds from the Demiurge's preoccupation with the administration of the material cosmos. Forgetting its intelligible and contemplative nature, the Demiurge disperses into the third god, and as a result, becomes bound up with the material world.

The First God, who exists in himself, is simple; for as he absolutely deals with none but himself, he is in no way divisible; however, the Second and Third God are One. When however this (unity) is brought together with Matter, which is Doubleness, the One Divinity indeed unites it, but is by Matter split, inasmuch as Matter is full of desires, and in a flowing condition. But inasmuch as he is not only in relation with the Intelligible, which would be more suitable to his own nature, he forgets himself, while he gazes on Matter, and cares for it. He comes into touch with the Perceptible, and busies himself with it; he leads it up into his own nature, because he was moved by desires for Matter. [28]

The passages from Moderatus and Numenius just examined assume a greater significance when we consider the close connection which the Neopythagorean tradition posited between the Indefinite *Dyad* and *tolma*. In this sense, the *Dyad's* separation from the One might be viewed as an audacious drive toward otherness. John Rist provides a concise summary of the available evidence that the Neopythagoreans identified the *Dyad* with *tolma*:

> It is quite certain that the *Dyad*, the material cause, which so mysteri-ously arose from the One, was called τόλμα. Such terminology, as Henry and Schwyzer's *Testimonia* to *Ennead* 5, 1, 1 indicates, is expressly said to be Pythagorean by Plutarch (*de Iside* 381F) and by the author of the *Theologoumena Arithmeticae* (p. 7, 19, and p. 9, 5-6 de Falco); Proclus (in *Alcibiades* 104E, p. 60 Westerink) tells us that the Pythagoreans actually called procession τόλμα; a similar doctrine is attributed by Johannes Lydus to the followers of Pherecydes (*de mens.* 2, 7, p. 24, 12-13). [29]

As Rist further observes, the Neopythagorean identification of the *Dyad* with *tolma* implied that the emergence of plurality constitutes a sin.[30] As a result of this association, *tolma* assumed a significant metaphysical and a moral character. For, as we have seen, the *Dyad* had become a principle which underlies not only differentiation and multiplicity, but privation and evil as well. Once coupled with *tolma*, the *Dyad* assumed a dynamic connotation as a surging movement toward otherness and non-being. And as we shall see, this was exactly its import in Plotinus. The Neopythagorean heritage of Plotinian thought is evident in Plotinus's appellation of Nous or Intellect as the *Dyad*, the beginning of plurality, and hence deficiency. [31]

Tolma and the Alexandrian *Milieu*

Alexandrian writers of the first and second centuries, A.D. (both Christian and non-Christian) utilized *tolma*-language in a distinct theological context. In this intellectual tradition, *tolma* or analo-gous terminology implies a rebelliousness, audacity, or boldness which either precipitates a movement away from God or which motivates an overstepping of bounds beyond one's proper rank or station. (As an aside, some mention should be made here of the presence of *tolma*-language in the Greek New Testament, where the verb *tolmao* (τολμέω) is used in a manner similar to that found in Hellenic and Hellenistic writings. [32])

Tolma-language assumes a prominence in the Hellenized Judaism of Philo Judaeus. Philo posits a wide gulf between God and creatures: fallenness characterizes created being. Pride, or a desire to be God's equal, constitutes the beginning of sin.[33] These themes are prominent in those places where Philo discusses impiety or irreverence toward God. In the *De Opificio Mundi*, Philo focuses upon the audacity of those who declare that God does not exist; in the same treatise, he ascribes a shameless audacity to those who respect creation more than God; in the *De Somniis*, he condemns those who dare to compare themselves to God.[34] Philo also uses *tolma*-language as a means of designating an insolent or indiscreet curiosity. In this context, curiosity assumes a pejorative connotation, insofar as it prompts one to penetrate those mysteries beyond the proper ken of humans:

> Why do you venture to determine the indeterminate (τί δε περὶ τῶν ἀτεκμάρτων τεκμαίρεσθαι τολμᾶς)? And why are you so busy with what you ought to leave alone, the things above? [35]

A similar line of thought is found in the writings of Clement, who uses *tolma*-language in a Christian context. In the *Stromateis*, such terminology designates an act of criminal audacity, whereby Philosophy itself is depicted as proceeding from a boldness that Divine Providence turns to our advantage.

> . . . Philosophy . . . was not sent by the Lord, but came stolen, or given by a thief. It was . . . some power or angel that had learned something of the truth . . . For the theft which reached men . . . had some advantage . . . but Providence directed the issue of the audacious deed to utility (δε εἰς το σθυθέρον τῆς προυίας τὴν εκβασιν τοῦ τολμήματος). [36]

Although the third-century Christian theologian Origen made no explicit use of *tolma*-language (to my knowledge, at least), he deserves some mention in this survey of Alexandrian thinkers. Origen shared many ideas with other prominent Alexandrians, with the Gnostics (although he opposed those sects, as did Plotinus), and with the Hermeticists. This is especially evident in the *De Principiis* (*On First Principles*) and its theory of the fall of souls.[37] According to Origen, the fall was the result of a satiety (κόρος) or weariness with the contemplative life and a negligence (αμέλεια) or carelessness with spiritual concerns.[38] The soul's loss of spiritual intensity ultimately leads to a decline to an inferior mode of existence. The degree of the soul's descent is proportionate to the gravity of its fault. In this context, the term "κόρος" designates an idleness or boredom which weakens the soul's resolve and distracts it from its focus upon the Divine. It experiences a forgetfulness of the Father which results in a debasement and fall. The motives for the fall discussed by Origen closely resemble those found in certain Neopythagorean, Hermetic, and Gnostic systems.

Tolma and the Hermetic Literature

The body of philosophical and theological writings known as the *Hermetica* likewise employed *tolma*-language in designating a spirit of rebelliousness or audacity which is instrumental in precipitating a cosmic fall. The Hermetic literature encompasses various writings on magic, astrology, alchemy, philosophy (both Platonism and Stoicism) and a theology associated with Hermes Trismegistus, the Greek name for the Egyptian god Thoth. These writings are divided into three major groups: (1) the *Corpus Hermeticum* (or the *Poimandres*); (2) the *Alclepius*; and (3) the *Kore Kosmou* (or the *Revelations of Isis*).[39] In the broadest sense, the Hermetica was representative of a popularized Greek philosophy or, what Theiler described as a "proleterian Platonism."[40]

Like the Alexandrian writers considered above, the Hermeticists used *tolma*-language in a theological context, closely connecting this audacity with a restless, insolent curiosity in the investigation of divine matters. The *Kore Kosmou* explicitly refers to the sins which preceded the fall and the embodiment of souls. *Kore Kosmou XXIV* partially attributes the soul's sin to an act of *tolma*. In this context, the soul's transgression lies in both audacity and curiosity (περίεργον ωπλίζοντο τόλμαν). The two errors are related ones: insolent curiosity proceeds from audacity and self-assertion beyond one's proper station. The souls' restless spirit motivates them to leave their designated place and begin a ceaseless movement. In the process, they attempt to penetrate and understand the Father's works. [41]

These same sentiments emerge in a later passage (*Kore Kosmou XLIV-XLVI*), where the interplay of audacity (τόλμα) and curiosity (περίεργοω) is again prominent. The offense of the souls stems from a bold curiosity which extends them beyond their assigned rank in the hierarchy of creation.[42] A similar theme is found in the *Poimandres*, which describes the fall of Anthropos, who wished to create on his own (ἠβουλήθη καὶ αυτὰς δημιαυργεῖν).[43] This theme receives additional treatment in the Gnostic writings, where the fall of the Aeon Sophia is attributed to a desire to create in imitation of God.

Tolma and Gnosticism

In the Christian and semi-Christian Gnostic systems of the second and third centuries, A.D., *tolma* assumed a prominent role, expressing an audacious desire for the Divine prerogative. E.R. Dodds has aptly characterized this period as an "Age of Anxiety," a time of intense insecurity and widespread uncertainty.[44] The limited scope of this chapter permits little more than a broad survey of the Gnostic tradition. My chief concern here lies in those systems which employed *tolma* or related language in connection with fall accounts. But let us first examine the more salient features of Gnosticism itself.

Because of the diversity of its teachings, it is rather difficult to formulate a comprehensive definition of the term "Gnosticism." Gnosticism has been described as an outgrowth of the syncretism that characterized the Hellenistic world, rather than a mere deviation from orthodox Christianity.[45] In this connection, a convenient summary of its mainlines is provided by C.J. De Vogel in her source-book of Hellenistic and Roman philosophy. According to De Vogel, the idea of a transcendent Godhead, a dualism of spirit and matter, a hierarchy of being, and a redemption of the spiritual nature of humans were prominent features of Gnostic systems.[46]

On the one hand, the "Gnostic" adhered to the belief that salvation is attainable only by means of a special revelatory knowledge or *gnosis*; on the other hand, the "Gnostic" felt alienated from a cosmos that was perceived as an evil place, precisely because it was the by-product of some upheaval or disorder on a broad scale.[47] Such pessimism fostered a widespread preoccupation with the human condition and its origins. Proceeding from the idea of a first principle of unity and perfection, Gnostics raised this key question: how could such a principle produce anything other than itself, and why would its product be so imperfect?[48] Generally speaking, the Gnostics attempted to explain the origin of the cosmos by means of the fall account. Some accounts of this type posited a transgression or deliberate act of impiety within the spiritual order. Others maintained that evil arises because a lower part of creation makes itself independent of a higher principle.[49] Such themes are prominent in the radically dualistic systems of Valentinus, Marcion, Bardesanes, and Mani.[50]

Tolma assumed an especially pronounced role in Valentinian Gnosticism. Both Irenaeus (*Adversus Haereses* I) and Hippolytus (*Refutatio VI*, 29-36) comment upon the fall of Sophia as described by the Valentinians. In the various versions of the myth which are available to us, Sophia's transgression lay in an attempt to penetrate the mystery of the Godhead or, in the desire to imitate the creative power of the Father.[51] In the most frequently quoted version (provided by Irenaeus), Sophia (the youngest of the Aeons within the spiritual Pleroma), was consumed by a passion or desire to investigate the Divine nature. In overstepping her bounds, Sophia fell, thereby producing the material cosmos. Irenaeus designates this passion or desire as *tolma*.

> But there rushed forth in advance of the rest that Aeon who was...the youngest...namely, Sophia, and suffered passion apart from the embrace of her consort Theleotos. This passion, they say, consisted in a desire to search into the nature of the Father; for she wished...to comprehend his greatness.[52]

The Nag Hammadi library (discovered in Upper Egypt in 1945) has opened up a whole new dimension of research in Gnosticism. In this body of works, we find motifs, imagery, and terminology that is consistent with Valentinianism. In this respect, the Nag Hammadi writings provide additional Gnostic sources for *tolma* (and related language). Interestingly, two of the treatises in the collection (i.e., *Zostrianos* and *Allogenes*) were apparently cited by Plotinus's disciple Porphyry (*Vita Plotini* 16) as writings composed by individuals in Plotinus's own circle that he attacked in his extended polemic "*Against the Gnostics*."[53] I will say more about this issue in due course (i.e., in *Chapter VI*, below). At present, let us consider some of the salient references to *tolma* or, alternately, *authadeia* (αὐθάδεια) in the context of Nag Hammadi fall accounts. At the outset, it should be noted that the Nag Hammadi library encompasses a series of Coptic translations of Greek manuscripts. Accordingly, these translations are rather rich in Greek loan words. In the survey which follows, I will focus upon those passages which employ the Coptic equivalents of *tolma* and *authades* in discussions of the fall of Sophia or her offspring.[54]

In *The Hypostasis of the Archons* (an exegesis on *Genesis 1-6*), the angel Eleleth discourses upon the generation of the archonic powers. In this revelatory narrative, Pistis-Sophia desires to create something on her own, without the aid of her consort (93:34-94:24). The product of this creation, we are told, was immersed in the "shadowy veil" of matter which exists apart from the celestial realm. Sophia's offspring thus takes on a form that was shaped from this substrate and undergoes a transformation into an arrogant (*authades*) lion-like beast.[55] Confronting the limitlessness of matter, Sophia's arrogant creature was guilty of a kind of blasphemy, claiming to be none other than God. According to the narrative, this act of self-exaltation constitutes a sin against the totality of things.[56]

An amplification of these ideas is found in the closely related *Treatise Without a Title on the Origin of the World*. There, we learn more about the transgression of the leonine Yaldabaoth (the first ruler that was generated by the creative desire of Pistis-Sophia). Here, Yaldabaoth's mistaken belief that he is God coincides with an ignorance of his origins and the rash assumption that he alone exists.[57] As a punishment for this arrogance, Sophia elevates a primal man of light above Yaldabaoth. An act of *tolma* is now imputed to Yaldabaoth, both for his reckless action and his scoffing of the prospect of condemnation.[58] A similar theme emerges in *The Second Treatise of the Great Seth*, where the archons surrounding Yaldabaoth display a daring (*tolma*) to be disobedient out of an ignorance of truth. [59]

Another version of the Myth of Sophia is found in *The Exegesis on the Soul*. In that work, Sophia is depicted as passing from an asexual, androgynous condition to a sexual one. This transformation is an expression of Sophia's fall into the body and the assumption of its accompanying ills. But once embodied, she is defiled by a host of assailants and discarded. Sophia then enters into a life of promiscuity, prostituting herself among many lovers. In effect, Sophia's entry into human existence and the abandonment of her proper home are portrayed in terms of a debasement. In this context, however, it is Sophia's lack of a spirit of *tolma* that is deemed problematic: in her shame, we are told, she no longer dares to leave those who violate her. [60]

Affinities with Valentinian Gnosticism are also found in *The Apocryphon of John*. According to this account, the aeon Sophia conceived a thought from within herself. Once projecting her image outward, she dared not turn back, but moved to and fro in the darkness of unknowing.[61] As in other treatises, Sophia's offspring exhibits an arrogance and ignorance of his origins. Such traits prompt a spirit of willfulness (*authades*) and a sense of autonomy.[62] Once again, Yaldabaoth's error is rooted in a refusal to acknowledge his derived status. By setting himself apart from all other things, he refuses to participate in reality as a whole and presumptuously imparts to himself a special, privileged position.

In the Nag Hammadi writings just considered, *tolma* and *authades* appear as expressions of a spirit of rebelliousness that proceeds from the involvement of Sophia or her offspring with lower levels of reality. In the *Zostrianos*, *tolma* is posited as the direct cause of certain aeons' association with material existence. In this work, we find an account of Zostrianos's heavenly ascent and reception of *gnosis* at various levels of the celestial regions. As the account unfolds, Zostrianos (a figure linked with the Persian prophet-reformer Zoroaster or Zarathustra) receives *gnosis* on the basis of his questions to spiritual guides or angels who lead him through the heavens. In this context, a key question which emerges concerns the origin of the world: how did such a world proceed from an immaterial, immutable source?

Zostrianos presents us with a triadic structure of reality, wherein Spirit occupies the highest position, the thought of Spirit (the Barbelo-aeon system) constitutes the second highest rank, and the material world and its being represents the inferior region of ignorance. There is a further triadic division of the Barbelo system into three aeons: Kalyptos (uppermost and hidden); the Protophanes (the first visible aeon); the Autogenes (self-generated aeon). In this hierarchical scheme, Spirit provides the ultimate source from which everything emanates. Each lower level is derived from that which exists above it. But a dualistic view of reality is apparent, with a tension between the spiritual and the material orders.

In *Zostrianos*, an explicit use of *tolma*-language emerges in the context of a discussion of the aeons' associated with Autogenes, the lowest aeon in the Barbelo-system and the one most proximate to the material world. We are told that those lower aeons confined to matter were left in that realm, and further, that they will pass away as a result of their ignorance of God.[63] But their coming into being is imputed to three factors: a knowledge of greatness, audacity (*tolma*), and power. [64]

These various expressions of the Myth of Sophia exhibit some apparent similarities with the creation and fall accounts of the *Hermetica* and the speculative systems of the Neopythagoreans. All of these schemes posit the sort of hierarchical structure which Jonas characterizes as a great, vertical "chain of being" proceeding downward from a principle of unity and perfection to a world of plurality and imperfection.[65] This downward movement, constituting a fall, serves to explain the apparent disparity between our world and the spiritual order.

As already noted, an important issue which emerges in these diverse schemes concerns the origin of evil. In a number of presentations, evil originates as the result of the attempted usurpation of divine authority. This theme is found in the Hermetic *Kore Kosmou* (where *tolma* is used in conjunction with *periergos*), in the *Poimandres*, and in Gnostic systems. In these places, a recurrent idea is that cosmic error lies in an arrogant desire to imitate the work of God.[66] Plotinus apparently refers to such dualistic creation accounts when he denies (in *Ennead* II.9) that the world is created out of "arrogance and audacity" (πῶς δι᾽ ἀλαζονείαν καὶ τόλμαν ποιεῖ;). Scholars support the contention that Plotinus was here addressing himself specifically to the Valentinians.[67]

Summation: The Sources of Plotinian *Tolma*

The substantive *tolma*, as well as its verb and adjectival forms, were widely employed in the literature, philosophy, and theology of the Hellenic and the Hellenistic traditions. By the third-century, A.D., *tolma*-language had acquired a variety of connotations as a result of its filtering through the classical authors, Plato, the Neopythagoreans, Middle Platonists, the Alexandrian writers, the Hermeticists, and the Gnostics. Such a widespread use and application, however, lent a tremendous ambiguity to the terminology.

In the classical authors, *tolma* expressed the very best attributes of gods and mankind alike: courage, daring, and endurance before the sometimes harsh decrees of Fate and cosmic Necessity. Gradually, *tolma* assumed a pejorative meaning when it came to express the ideas of rebelliousness, an overstepping of bounds, and a defiance in the face of divine authority. In Plato, *tolma*-language was used in a rather ironic sense to designate a brashness or "pluck" in challenging widely accepted philosophical norms or time-honored teachings. In Neopythagoreanism, *tolma* acquired a whole new set of metaphysical connotations: once it was identified with the Indefinite *Dyad*, the term expressed a dynamic will toward otherness and plurality. By designating the *Dyad* as *tolma*, the Neopythagoreans connected it with the notions of procession, emanation, and multiplicity. In this respect, *tolma* assumed the role of a principle of generation which stands in opposition to the One's primal unity.

While the Neopythagoreans employed *tolma*-language on a metaphysical plane, the Alexandrians (i.e., Philo and Clement), Hermeticists, and Gnostics used it in a theological context. These groups of thinkers exhibit the syncretic tendency characteristic of Hellenistic thought and shared in common various ideas. Each group attempted to account for evil by means of fall accounts which posit some sin or transgression as the cause of the present condition of the cosmos. Such a transgression might proceed from a rash overstepping of one's bounds, an attempted usurpation of Divine authority, a seizure of the Divine prerogative, or an insolent curiosity.

The various contexts in which we have encountered the use of *tolma*-language demonstrate that this terminology carries with it an extremely rich heritage. In analyzing the meaning of the term (and its variants) in Plotinus's *Enneads,* such an historical background must be borne in mind. For as we have seen, *tolma* not only assumed a profound metaphysical significance, but became surrounded by a plethora of theological, moral, and psychological connotations as well.

Notes

1. Major Plotinian passages containing the use of *tolma* or related language are as follows: (a) for *Nous–Ennead* VI.9(9).5.24-29: ". . . not dividing itself by virtue of its nearness next after the One, but somehow it desired to stand apart from the One with audacity" (τῷ πλησίον μετὰ τὸ ἕν εἶναι, ἀποστῆναι δέ πως του ἑνὸς τολμήσας); *Ennead* I.8(51).9.18-19: "This intellect which looks at matter is another intellect that is not intellect, since it dares to see what is not its own" (Διὸ καὶ νοῦς ἄλλος οὗτος, οὐ νοῦς, τολμήσας ιδεῖν τὰ μη αυτοῦ); (b) for individual souls—*Ennead* V.1(10).1.3-5: "The origin of evil for them is *tolma*" (Ἀρχὴ μεν οὖν αὐταῖς του κακοῦ ἡ τόλμα); *Ennead* V.2(11).2.5-7: "When therefore, the soul becomes a plant, what is in the plant is another part of it of sorts, the most audacious and foolish part of it and that which has advanced to this extent" (. . . τὸ τολμηρότατον καὶ αφρονεστάτον καὶ προεληλυθὸς μέχρι τοσούτον).

2. A.H. Armstrong, *The Cambridge History of Later Greek and Early Medieval Philosophy* (Cambridge, 1970), p. 242: "This is the idea which appears in a few passages, that the original giving-out of the indeterminate vitality, the 'indefinite *dyad*' which is the basis of Intellect from the One, and the giving out of Soul from Intellect which is the next stage in the 'unfolding' of derived being and depends upon the first, are acts of illegitimate self-assertion (τόλμα). All existence, in this way of looking at it, depends on a special kind of radical original sin, a wish for separation and independence . . ."
   Naguib Baladi, "Origine et Signification de l'Audace chez Plotin," *Le Néoplatonisme* (Royaumant, 1971), p. 89: "En tout cela, l'audace est essentiellement liée a la séparation et a alterite."
   For the sake of simplicity, the phrase "*tolma*-language" will be used throughout this study as a means of designating the substantive *tolma*, one of its verb forms, or an adjectival form.

3. As Armstrong states (in "Gnosis and Greek Philosophy," *Gnosis, Festschrift für Hans Jonas*, Göttingen, 1978, p. 116), an essential point has already been made by scholars, namely, that Plotinus's use of *tolma* has behind it a "clearly demonstrable history."

4. William Chase Greene, *Moira: Fate, Good, and Evil in Greek Thought* (Cambridge, Mass.: Harvard University Press, 1944), p. 46. Characterizing the literature of this early period in Greek history, Greene writes of a "single tradition from Homer to Theognis and beyond, drawing from

heroic action, peasant and civic life, and personal vicissitudes its touch of reality . . . (coming) to distrust Nature and the gifts of the gods, and to find whatever of good the world affords more in social justice and the wise and brave acceptance and use of what Fate brings."

5. Liddell and Scott, *Greek-English Lexicon* (Oxford, 1953), p. 1803. Some Homeric passages displaying *tolma*-language in this context are *Iliad* 10, 205; 10, 232; 12, 51; *Odyssey* 17, 284; 24, 162-163.

6. E.R. Dodds, *The Greeks and the Irrational* (Berkeley and Los Angeles: University of California Press, 1973), p. 29: "When we turn from Homer to the fragmentary literature of the Archaic Age, and to those writers of the Classical Age who still preserve the archaic outlook—as do Pindar and Sophocles, and to a great extent Herodotus—one of the first things that strikes us is the deepened awareness of human insecurity and human helplessness . . . which has its religious correlate in the feeling of divine hostility . . . in the sense that an overmastering Power and Wisdom forever holds Man down, keeps him from rising above his station."

7. Examples are found in Theognis, fragments 355; 591; 1029. cf. Pindar, *Nemean Odes* 7, 59; *Olypmian Odes* 9, 82.

8. For examples of the use of *tolma*-language within the context of Greek tragedy, see: Aeschylus, *Prometheus* 16; 235-236; *Choephori* 996; Sophocles, *Philoctetes* 82; Euripides, *Iphigenia in Taurus* 110. Greene describes the whole thrust of Greek tragedy in these terms (*Moira: Fate, Good, and Evil in Greek Thought*, p. 91): ". . . the finest and most profound tragic effect comes when the poet is not content merely to set forth external events, nor even the fact of guilt, but exhibits also the moral attitude of his protagonist towards events and towards his own action. He answers the call to honor, come what may; he endures what fate or the gods send."

9. Plato, *Sophist* 258d-e (trans. Hamilton and Cairns, Princeton, 1973). As pointed out by Paul Seligman (*Being and Non-Being*, The Hague: Martinus Nijhoff, 1974, p. 85), the "Stranger" has not discussed non-being, but has attempted to define its very nature in terms of difference.

10. Plato, *Theaetetus* 197a (trans. Hamilton and Cairns, Princeton, 1973). cf. *Meno* 71b3-8; John McDowell, in notes to his translation of Plato's *Theaetetus* (Oxford, 1973), p. 219.

11. The theme of Socratic Ignorance is presented in Plato's *Apology* 29, trans. Benjamin Jowett (Oxford, 1953): "Is not this ignorance of a disgraceful sort, the ignorance which is the conceit that a man knows what he does not know?"

12. W.R. Inge, *The Philosophy of Plotinus*, volume I (London: Longmans, Green, and Co., 1923), p. 83. Lectures IV and V of this collection ("Forerunners of Plotinus," pp. 71-121) provide a still excellent survey of

the philosophical antecedents of Plotinus. For an extremely detailed analysis of this period (proceeding from the Old Academy and Aristotle to the later Academy and the Pythagoreans, the Peripatos, and the Stoa), see Philip Merlan's contribution to *The Cambridge History of Later Greek and Early Medieval Philosophy*, pp. 53-106.

13. R.T. Wallis, *Neoplatonism* (New York: Charles Scribner's Sons, 1972), pp. 32-33. Thomas Whittaker, *The Neoplatonists* (Cambridge, 1912), p. 36.

14. B.A.G. Fuller, *The Problem of Evil in Plotinus* (Cambridge, 1912), p. 36.

15. A.H. Armstrong, "Gnosis and Greek Philosophy," p. 95. Armstrong distinguishes the spirit of world-alienation characterizing the Platonic/Pythagorean tradition from that of its Gnostic counterparts: "... for the Platonist or Pythagorean our lower world ... is predominately a good world. It really is a cosmos, a thing of beauty and order ... There can be no question of total rejection of the world or a spirit of revolt against its makers ..."

16. Aristotle, *Metaphysics* I 6, 987a 29ff.

17. e.g. Plato's *Philebus* 26E-30E.

18. cf. John Dillon's discussion in *The Middle Platonists* (London: Duckworth & Co., Ltd., 1977), pp. 3-4.

19. John Dillon, *The Middle Platonists*, p. 45.

20. In Aristotle, Metaphysics N I, 1087b49 (fr. 48b Lang): οἱ δὲ τὸ ἕτερον τῶν ἐναντίων ὕλην ποιοῦσιν, οἱ μὲν τῷ ἑνὶ τῷ ἑνὶ τῷ ἴσῳ τὸ ἄνισον, ὡς τοῦτο τὴν τοῦ πλήθους οὖσαν φύσιν, οἱ δὲ τῷ ἑνὶ πλῆθος. γεννῶνται γὰρ οἱ ἀριθμοὶ τοῖς μὲν εκ τῆς ἀνίσου δυάδος τοῦ μεγάλου καὶ μικροῦ, τῷ δ ἐκ τοῦ πλήθους, ὑπὸ τῆς τοῦ ἑνὸς δὲ οὐσίας ἀμφοῖν.

21. In Aetius, *Plac.* I 7, 30; *Dox.* p. 304b1 (fr. 15H., first part): Θεοκράτης Ἀγαθήνορος καλχηδόνιος τὴν μονάδα καὶ δυάδα θεούς, τὴν μὲν ὡς ἄρρενα πατρὸς ἔχουσαν τάξιν ἐν οὐρανῷ βασιλεύουσαν, ἥντινα προσαγορεύει καὶ Ζῆνα καὶ περιττὸν καὶ νοῦν, ὅστις ἐστὶν αὐτῷ πρῶτος θεός· τὴν δὲ ὡς θήλειαν, μητρὸς θεῶν δίκην, τῆς ὑπὸ τὸν οὐρανὸν λήξεως ἡγουμένην, ἥτις ἐστὶν αὐτῷ ψυχὴ τοῦ παντός.

22. Plutarch of Chaeronea, *De defectu oraculorum* 428Eff.: ἐκεῖνο δ᾽ ἤδη σκοπεῖτε κοινῇ προσέχοντες, ὅτι τῶν ἀνωτάτων αχων, λέγω δὲ τοῦ ἑνὸς καὶ τῆς ἀορίστου δυάδος, ἡ μὲν ἀμορφίας πάσης στοιχεῖον οὖσα καὶ ἀταξίας ἀπειρία κέκληται· ἡ δὲ τοῦ ἑνὸς φύσις ὁρίζουσα καὶ καταλαμβάνουσα τῆς ἀπειρίας τὸ κενὸν καὶ ἄλογον καὶ ἀόριστον ἔμμορφον παρέχεται καὶ τὴν ἑπομένην <τῃ> περὶ τὰ αἰσθητὰ δόξῃ κατηγόρευσιν ἀμωσγέπως ὑπομένον καὶ δεχόμενον.

23. Discussing this passage, Armstrong ("Gnosis and Greek Philosophy," p. 117) maintains: "We learn that the primal One, the "Unitary Logos," wishing to produce from himself the origin of beings, by self-privation made room for indefinite formless quantity, which is the *Dyad*, the principle on which the Demiurge works to produce in the world in the *Timaeus*, the ultimate origin of evil."

24. Simplicius, *In Phys.* 230, 34-231, 27 Diels. I rely here upon the translation presented by Philip Merlan in *The Cambridge History of Later Greek and Early Medieval Philosophy*, pp. 91-92. Merlan also provides a complete quotation of the original Greek text.

25. John Dillon, *The Middle Platonists*, p. 348.

26. E.R. Dodds, "Numenius and Ammonius," *Les Sources de Plotin* (Entriens Hardt: Vandoeuvres-Geneve, 1957), p. 23.

27. Frederick C. Copleston, S.J., *A History of Philosophy*, volume I, part 2 (Garden City, New York: Image Books, 1962), pp. 191-192.

28. Numenius, fragment XXVI (in *The Neoplatonic Writings of Numenius*, Collected and Translated from the Greek by Kenneth Guthrie (Lawrence, Kansas: Selene Books, 1987), pp. 26-29: Ὁ θεὸς ὁ μὲν πρῶτος εν ἑαυτῷ ὤν εστιν ἁπλοῦς, διὰ τὸ ἑαυτῷ συγγιγνόμενος διόλου μή ποτε ειναι διαιρετός· ὁ θεὸς μέντοι ὁ δεύτερος καὶ τρίτος ἐστὶν εἷς· συμφερόμενος δὲ τῇ ὕλῃ δυάδι οὔσῃ ἑνοῖ αὐτήν, σχίζεται δὲ ὑπ᾽ αὐτῆς, ἐπιθυμητικὸν ἦθος ἐχούσης καὶ ῥεούσης. τῷ οὖν μὴ εἶναι πρὸς τῷ νοητῷ (ἡν γὰρ ἂν πρὸς ἑαυτῷ), διὰ τὸ τὴν ὕλην βλέπειν ταύτης ἐπιμελούμενος ἀπερίοπτος ἑαυτοῦ γίνεται, καὶ ἅπτεται τοῦ αἰσθητοῦ καὶ περιέπει, ἀνάγει ετ ἔτι εἰς τὸ ἴδιον ἦθοω, ἐπορεξάμενος τῆς ὕλης.

29. John M. Rist, "Monism: Plotinus and Some Predecessors," *Harvard Studies in Classical Philology* 70 (1965): 338.

30. This is consistent with Plotinus's statement in *Ennead* III.8(30).8, 32-36 that it would have been better if Nous had never become second to the primal unity of the One. Cornford ("Mysticism and Science in the Pythagorean Tradition," *The Classical Quarterly* XVII: 6) describes this development in these terms: ". . . later mysticism regards the emergence of the Dyad as an act of rebellious audacity."

31. *Ennead* V.1(10).5.13-14: "The number . . . and *Dyad* . . . are generative principles and intellect (ὁ οὖν ἐκεῖ λεγόμενος ἀριθμὸς καὶ ἡ δυὰς λόγοι καὶ νους)."
    cf. Naguib Baladi, *La Pensee de Plotin*, p. 13: "Si après Plotin, c'est de l'Un que l'être ou l'intelligence surgit par audace, ce sont les pythagoriciens qui passent pour avoir été les premiers à employer ce terme dans un sens tout a fait proche."

32. cf. *Romans* 5:7; 15, 18; *Matthew* 22-46; Luke 20:40.

33. Henry Chadwick, "Philo and the Beginnings of Christian Thought," *The Cambridge History of Later Greek and Early Medieval Philosophy*, p. 145. cf. Philo Judaeus, *Legum Allegoriae* I, 49; *De Cherubim* 58-64.

34. Philo Judaeus, *De Opificio Mundi* 170; 45; *De Somniis* II, 130.

35. Philo Judaeus, *De Somniis* I, 54.
     cf. *Heres* 240 (where *koros* is said to overcome souls);
     De Opificio Mundi 168 (which speaks of the twin evils of idleness and satiety).

36. Clement of Alexandria, *Stromateis* I, 81; VI, 16 (*Anti-Nicene Fathers*, Grand Rapids, Michigan, 1951).

37. Origen, *De Principiis* I,3.8; I,4.1; I,6.2; I,7,5; I,8.1; I,8.41; II,8.3; III,1.13.
     I provide a fuller discussion of *koros* in the context of Origen's account of the Fall in "Satiety and the Fall of Souls in Origen's *De Principiis*," *Studia Patristica*, XVIII-3: 455-462. For a discussion of *koros* in Origen against the background of its place in Patristic and classical thought, see Marguerite Harl, "Recherches sur l'origenisme d'Origène: la 'satiété' (κόρος) de la contemplation comme motif de la chute des âmes," *Studia Patristica* (VII, Part II): 373-405.

38. Origen, *De Principiis* II,8.3; III,1.13.

39. G.W. MacRae, "Hermetic Literature," *New Catholic Encyclopedia* (1967 edition), volume VI: 1076-1077.

40. A.H. Armstrong, "Gnosis and Greek Philosophy," p. 89.

41. J. Zandee, *The Terminology of Plotinus and of Some Gnostic Writings, Mainly the Fourth Treatise of the Jung Codex* (Istanbul, 1961), p. 27.
     cf. A.J. Festugiere, *La Revelation d'Hermes Trismegiste* III (Paris, 1953), p. 83: "Et ces ames, comme si elles avaient accompli un exploit, d'ores et déjà s'armaient d'une audace indiscrète (oú d'une curiosité insolentè, περίεργον ὡπλόζοντο τόλμαν, et transgressaient les commandements; elles quittant maintenant leurs propres sections et depots et ne consentaient plus à demeurer en un seul lieu, mais ne cessaient de se mouvoir: continuer d'être attachées a une seule residence, elles le regardainet comme une mort."

42. Festugiere, III, p. 84: "L'expression reparaît dans le discours où Momus blâme Hermès d'avoir créé l'homme (46—ἐιτα οὐ καὶ μέχρις οὐρανοῦ περίεργον ὁπλιοθήσονται τόλμαν) et les deux notions de περίεργια et de τόλμα constamment associees dans ce meme passage: l'homme sera περίεργος ἀφθαλμοῖς (44), il pretendra ὁρᾶν τόλμηρῶς les beaux mysteres de la nature (ib.), il éntendra τολμησὰς χεῖρας pour rechercher

(ἐπὶ ζήτησιν) ce qui est par delà les mers (45). Il faut donc que l'homme devienne l'esclave des passions et qu'ainsi la curiosité indiscrète de l'ame humaine (τῶν ψυχῶν αὐτῶν τὸ περίεργον) soit desappointee dans son attente. Maintenant, si l'homme est ainsi περίεργος et τολμηρός c'est evidemment en raison de son âme: le péché originel de l'ame a sa repercussion dans le composé de corps et d'âme."

43. *Poimandres* 10, 20.
     cf. A.J. Festugiere, III, p. 89: "Dans son désir même de créer, l'Anthropôs commence sa chute. La suite le manifeste tout aussitôt."

44. The phrase is taken from Dodds' *Pagan and Christian In An Age of Anxiety* (Cambridge, 1968), a concise work which presents an excellent survey of the intellectual climate of the period in question. Dodds believed that the spirit of pessimism and alienation was not confined to the Gnostic movement alone, but even penetrated the educated circles of pagan Hellenistic culture. (Marcus Aurelius's *Meditations* provides a case in point.) As Dodds asserts (p. 35), ". . . the contempt for the human condition and hatred of the body was a disease endemic in the entire culture of the period."

45. R.McI. Wilson, *The Gnostic Problem* (London: A.R. Mowbray and Co., Ltd., 1958), p. 116. M. Puech refers to this particular problem in "Plotin et les Gnostiques," *Les Sources de Plotin* (Foundation Hardt: Geneve, 1960), p. 162: "Les diverses sectes gnostiques ont pu se faire des emprunts mutuels, voire fusionner entre elles. Les livres s'echangaient d'un groupe à l'autre; toute une littérature ésotérique a circulé, qui est devenue un bien commun ou a été adoptee par tel ou tel conventicule dans un esprit très éclectique et sans souci de l'origine du volume accueilli."

46. C.J. De Vogel, *Greek Philosophy*, volume III (Leiden: E.J. Brill, 1959), pp. 407-408. Hans Jonas also presents a fine summary of the main features of this phenomenon in *The Gnostic Religion* (Boston, 1963), pp. 31-32: "First, all of the phenomena which we noted in connection with the 'oriental wave' are of a decidedly religious nature; and this . . . is the prominent characteristic of the second phase of Hellenistic culture in general. Second, all these currents have in some way to do with salvation: the general religion of the period is a religion of salvation. Third, all of them exhibit an exceedingly transcendent (i.e., transmundane) conception of God and in connection with it an equally transcendent and otherworldly idea of the goal of salvation. Finally, they maintain a radical dualism of realms of being . . . and . . . an extreme polarization of existence affecting . . . reality as a whole . . ."

47. G.W. MacRae, "Gnosticism," *New Catholic Encyclopedia* (1967 edition), volume VI: 523; A.H. Armstrong, "Gnosis and Greek Philosophy," p. 89.

48. John Dillon, "The Descent of the Soul in Middle Platonism and Gnostic Theory," *The Rediscovery of Gnosticism*, volume I (Leiden: E.J. Brill, 1980),

p. 357: "Accepting that a world or universe of some sort is thus brought into being, how can we further explain the imperfect and disorderly nature of our world as it now exists? Something surely, has gone wrong somewhere. There must at some state, over and above the basic creation, have been a declination or Fall."

49. J. Zandee, p. 26. This theme is also reflected in Irenaeus's *Adversus Haereses* (I, 29, 4), which discusses the "Barbelo Gnostic" account depicting the agitated Sophia-Prunicus's production of a work in which there was found ignorance and audacity.

50. E.R. Dodds, *Pagan and Christian In An Age of Anxiety*, p. 24. The notion of the fallen soul ultimately has its roots in the Orphic and Pythagorean traditions, each of which viewed embodiment as a form of punishment. This influence is visible in Plato's myth of the soul's descent into the body (*Phaedrus* 246); through Plato, the theme appears to have entered the mainstream of Greek thought.

51. Sophia played an important role in various Gnostic systems, including that of the Valentinians. As Puech observes ("Plotin et les Gnostiques," pp. 162-163): ". . . Sophia n'est pas une Entité propre au seul valentisme: elle appartient aussi a des systemes de gnose tres probablement antérieurs à celui de Valentin et similiares ou identiques à ceux des Barbélognostiques . . ."
cf. G.C. Stead, "The Valentinian Myth of Sophia," *The Journal of Theological Studies* (New Series) 20 (1969): 78.

52. Irenaeus, *Adv. Haereses I*, 2.2 (Trans. Roberts and Rambaud (The Writings of Irenaeus), volume I, Edinburgh, 1884.). Προήλατο δὲ πολὺ ὁ τελευταῖος καὶ νεώτατος τῆς δωδεκάδος, τῆς ὑπὸ τοῦ Ἀνθρώπου καὶ τῆς Ἐκκλησίας, προβεβλημένος Αἰών, τουτέστιν ἡ Σοφία, καὶ ἔπαθε πάθος ἄνευ τῆς ἐπιπλοκῆς τοῦ ζυγοῦ τοῦ Θελητοῦ· ὃ ἐνήρξατο μὲν ἐν τοῖς περὶ τὸν Νοῦν καὶ τὴν Ἀλήθειαν, ἀπέσκηψε δ' εἰς τοῦτον τὸν παρατραπέντα, πρόφασιν μὲν ἀγάπης, τόλμης δέ, διὰ τὸ μὴ κεκοινωνῆσθαι τῷ Πατρὶ τῷ τελείῳ, καθὼς καὶ ὁ Νοῦς. Τὸ δὲ πάθος εἶναι ζήτησιν τοῦ Πατρός· ἤθελε γάρ, ὡς λέγουσι, τὸ μέγεθος αὐτοῦ κατα λαβεῖν.

53. In addition to *Zostrianos and Allogenes* (both of which Porphyry explicitly mentions), other Nag Hammadi treatises have been proposed (namely, *Three Steles of Seth*, Nag Hammadi Codex VII,5 and *Marsanes*, Nag Hammadi Codex X) as likely candidates for the unspecified Gnostic sources to which he refers at *Vita Plotini* 16. For a discussion of this issue, see Birger A. Pearson's "The Tractate *Marsanes* (NHC X) and the Platonic Tradition," in *Gnosis*, a Festschrift für Hans Jonas (Göttingen: Vandenhoeck & Ruprecht, 1978), pp. 373-384.

54. For a critical treatment of these writings, see *The Nag Hammadi Codices*—Facsimiles/Translations/Commentaries/ Studies (Leiden: E.J.

Brill, 1971, ff.). For English translations of the Codices, also see *The Nag Hammadi Library in English*. Directed by J.M. Robinson and translated by members of the Coptic Gnostic Library Project of the Institute for Antiquity and Christianity. (Leiden: E.J. Brill, 1977).

55. *The Hypostasis of the Archons* 94:15 (NHC II,2-7):

αϥⲭιⲧⲩⲡⲟⲥ ⲉⲃⲟⲗ ⲍⲛ̄ ⲑⲁⲉⲓⲃⲉⲥ αϥⲱ ⲱⲡⲉ ⲛⲟⲩⲑⲏⲣⲓⲟⲛ ⲛⲁⲩⲑⲁⲇⲏⲥ ⲛ̄ⲛⲓⲛⲉ ⲙ̄ⲙⲟⲩⲉⲓ

56. *The Hypostasis of the Archons* 94:24 (NHC II,2-7):

αⲅⲱ ⲙⲛ̄ ϭⲉ αⲭⲛ̄ⲧ ⲛ̄ⲧⲁⲣⲉϥ ⲭⲉ ⲡⲁⲉⲓ αϥⲣ̄ ⲛⲟⲃⲉ ⲉⲍⲣⲁⲓ ⲉⲡⲧⲏⲣϥ

57. *Treatise Without Title on the Origin of the World* 103:23 (NHC II,2-7):
ⲡⲉⲭⲁϥ ⲭⲉ αⲛⲟⲕ ⲡⲉ ⲡⲛⲟⲩⲧⲉ αⲅⲱ ⲙⲛ̄ ⲕⲉⲟⲩα ϣⲟⲟⲡ αⲭⲛⲧ

58. *Treatise Without Title on the Origin of the World* 107:35 (NHC II,2-7):

ⲛ̄ⲧⲟϥ ⲇⲉ ⲍⲱⲥ αⲛⲟⲏⲧⲟⲥ αϥⲕⲁⲧⲁⲫⲣⲟⲛⲉⲓ ⲛ̄ⲧⲕⲁⲧⲁⲅⲛⲱⲥⲓⲥ αⲅⲱ αϥⲧⲟⲗⲙⲁ

59. *The Second Treatise of the Great Seth* 69:7-14 (NHC VII,2):

αⲅⲱ ⲉⲧⲃⲉ ⲡⲁⲓ αⲅⲟⲅⲱⲛ̄ⲍ ⲉⲃⲟⲗ ⲛ̄{ⲛ}ⲟⲩⲙⲟⲩⲭϭ ⲛ̄{ⲛ}ⲟⲩⲙ̄ⲛ̄ⲧ αⲧⲥⲟⲟⲩⲛ ⲍⲛ̄ ⲟⲩⲡⲁⲣα ⲡϣⲱⲗⲍ ⲛ̄ⲧⲉ ⲟⲩⲕⲣⲱⲙ · ⲙⲛ̄ ⲟⲩⲕⲁⲍ ⲙⲛ̄ ⲟⲩⲣⲉϥⲍⲱⲧⲃ̄ · ⲉⲍⲉⲛⲕⲟⲩⲉⲓ ⲛⲉ αⲅⲱ ⲛ̄αⲧⲥⲃⲱ · ⲉⲛⲥⲉⲥⲟⲟⲩⲛ αⲛ ⲉαⲩⲣ̄ ⲧⲟⲗⲙⲁ ⲉⲛαⲓ ·

60. *The Exegesis on the Soul* 128:13-14 (NHC II,2-7):

ⲉⲃⲟⲗ ⲇⲉ ⲙ̄ⲡϣ ⲓⲡⲉ ⲟⲩⲕⲉⲧⲓⲙⲁⲥⲧⲟⲗⲙⲁ ⲉⲕⲁⲁⲩ ⲛ̄ⲥⲱⲥ

61. *The Apocryphon of John* 36:16-37:2 (Berlin Papyrus 8502):

ⲧⲛ̄ϣⲃⲣ̄ ⲥⲱⲛⲉ ϭⲉ ⲧⲥⲟⲫⲓα ⲉⲅⲉ ⲱⲛ ⲧⲉ αⲥⲙⲉⲉⲩⲉ ⲉⲩⲙⲉⲉⲩⲉ ⲉⲃⲟⲗ ⲛ̄ⲍⲏⲧⲥ̄ αⲩⲱ ⲍⲣαⲓ ⲍⲙ ⲡⲙⲉⲉⲩⲉ ⲙⲡⲉⲡⲛ̄α ⲙⲛ̄ ⲡϣⲟⲣⲡ ⲛ̄ⲥⲟⲟⲩⲛ αⲥⲣ̄ⲍⲛαⲥ ⲉⲟⲩⲱⲛⲍ ⲙⲡⲓ[ⲛⲉ] ⲉⲃⲟⲗ ⲛⲍⲏⲧⲥ̄ ⲉⲙⲡⲉϥⲧⲱⲟⲩ

The Apocryphon of John 45:13-18 (Berlin Papyrus 8502):

αⲥⲙⲉⲧαⲛⲟⲉⲓ αⲅⲱ ⲉⲥⲛα ⲉⲥⲛⲏⲩ ⲍⲙ̄ ⲡⲕαⲕⲉ ⲛ̄ⲧⲙⲛ̄ⲧαⲧⲥⲟⲟⲩⲛ αⲥαⲣⲭⲉⲥⲑαⲓ ⲉϣⲓⲡⲉ αⲅⲱ ⲉⲛⲥⲧⲟⲗⲙα αⲛ ⲉⲕⲧⲟⲥ αⲗⲗα ⲛⲉⲥⲛα ⲉⲥⲛⲏⲩ ⲡⲉ ⲡⲉⲥⲛα ⲇⲉ ⲙⲛ̄ ⲡⲉⲥⲉⲓ ⲡαⲓ ⲡⲉ ⲉⲡⲓⲫⲉⲣⲉ

62. *The Apocryphon of John* 45:20-46 (Berlin Papyrus 8502):

ⲧαⲣⲉϥⲭⲓ ϭⲉ ⲛⲟⲩϭⲟⲙ ⲛ̄ϭⲓ ⲡαⲩⲑα [ⲇⲏⲥ ⲉⲃ] ⲟⲗ ⲍⲛ ⲧⲙααⲩ ⲛαϥⲟ ⲛ̄ⲛαⲧⲥⲟⲟⲩⲛ ⲛⲟⲩαⲧⲟ ⲉⲧⲉ ⲛⲉⲧⲟⲩⲟⲧⲃ̄ ⲉⲧⲉϥⲙααⲩ ·

63. *Zostrianos* 128:13-14 (NHC VIII,1):

    ⲁⲅⲱ ⲉⲧⲃⲉ ⲟⲩⲅⲛⲱ[ⲥ]ⲓⲥ ⲛⲧⲉ ⲟⲩⲙⲛⲧⲛⲟϭ ⲙⲛ ⲟⲩⲧⲟⲗⲙⲏ ⲁⲅⲱ ⲟⲩϭⲟⲙ
    ⲉⲁⲩ ϣⲱⲡⲉ ⲁⲅ ⲱ ⲁⲩⲥⲉⲗⲥⲱⲗⲟⲩ •

64. *Zostrianos* 128:10-13 (NHC XIII,1):

    ⲉⲁⲩⲣ ⲁⲧⲉⲓⲙⲉ ⲉ ⲡⲛⲟⲩⲧⲉ ⲥⲉⲛⲁⲃⲱ ⲗ ⲉⲃⲟⲗ •

    cf. *The Gospel of the Egyptians* III,61:16-23 (NHC III,2) which imputes (in a
    Christianized format) the error of the devil to an audacity (*tolma*) which
    prompted him, along with his powers and angels, to act against them-
    selves:

    ⲧⲟⲧⲉ ⲡⲛⲟϭ ⲛ̄ⲥⲏⲑ • ⲁϥⲛⲁⲩ ⲉⲧⲉⲛⲉⲣⲓⲁ ⲙ̄ⲡⲇⲓⲁⲃⲟⲗⲟⲥ ⲙ̄ⲛ ⲡⲉϥⲁⲧⲟ
    ⲛ̄ⲥⲙⲟⲧ ⲙ̄ⲛ ⲛⲉϥⲙⲉⲉⲩⲉ ⲉⲧⲛⲁ ϣⲱⲡⲉ ⲉϫⲛ̄ ⲧⲉϥⲅⲉⲛⲉⲁ ⲛ̄ⲁⲫⲑⲁⲣⲧⲟⲛ ⲉⲧⲉ
    ⲙⲉⲥⲕⲓⲙ ⲙ̄ⲛ ⲛ̄ⲇⲓⲱⲅⲙⲟⲥ ⲛ̄ⲛⲉϥϭⲟⲙ ⲙ̄ⲛ ⲛⲉϥⲁⲅⲅⲉⲗⲟⲥ ⲙ̄ⲛ ⲧⲉⲩⲡⲗⲁⲛⲏ
    ϫⲉ ⲁⲩⲧⲟⲗⲙⲁ ⲉⲣⲟⲟⲩ ⲙ̄ⲙⲓⲛ ⲙ̄ⲙⲟⲟⲩ •

65. Hans Jonas, "The Soul in Gnosticism and Plotinus," *Neoplatonisme*
    (Royaumant, 1971), p. 46.

66. Festugiere (III, p. 88) designates this desire as the origin of sin in such
    dualistic systems: ". . . dans les speculations gnostiques le théme 'desire
    de creer' a dû être considéré comme mauvais, il a dû figurer comme une
    sorte de péché originel, dès là qu'on ne peut creer sans matiere et que la
    matiere est mauvais. La notion d'un Démiurge non seulment inférieur au
    Premier Dieu, mais encore mauvais et, comme tel, opposé au Dieu
    Suprême est courante dans les gnoses dualistes. Et l'on peut donc penser
    que le désir de créer, dans un dualisme coherent est déjà, par lui-même,
    mauvais."

67. Puech argues this point in "Plotin et les Gnostiques," p. 174: "Il est, apres
    tout, fort possible que, comme certains indices porteraient a le croire, les
    sectaires connus a Rome par nos deux auteurs se soient appeles eux-
    memes, tout simplement, "Gnostiques" . . . De tout facon, une question
    devra etre posee et traitee: quelles etaient les relations de ces
    "Gnostiques" avec les Valentinians? Qu'une influence du valentinisme se
    soit exercee sur eux n's rien que de tres vraisemblable: Valentin a fait a
    Rome la majeure partie de sa carriere: il y a laisse ses ecrits; les auditeurs
    de Plotin ont pu fort bien les connaitre, et avant meme l'arrivee du
    philosophe dans le ville. Mais il se peut aussi qu'ils aient professe des
    doctrines qui se trouvaient etre, en fait, communes a leur ecole propre et
    a celle des Valentiniens."

Chapter II

Tolma and the Emergence of Nous

The second hypostasis in the intelligible universe of Plotinus is *Nous* or Intellect, the immediate product of the One's outpouring and consequently, the recipient of its infinite vitality. Among its diverse roles in Plotinus's scheme, *Nous* is an effect of the One's diffusiveness, constituting the initial actualization of the power of the One, the highest level of both human and universal intellect, the Intellectual Cosmos (or, in Platonic terms, the World of Forms), and a universe of spiritual realities united in noetic contemplation.

Plotinus characterizes *Nous* as a "many-in-one" or plurality in unity (*Ennead* VI.2(43).22.10-13). While it is derived from primal unity, it contains within itself a plurality of Forms. In this respect, *Nous* constitutes an intelligible world or universe of being in its own right (*Ennead* I.8(51).2.15-21). The Forms are the constituents of this intelligible world, distinct from each other, yet unified. As Plotinus affirms, *Nous* possesses all things and is all things. It is not the case that *Nous* is one reality and the universe another. It represents a great collectivity or aggregate of everything which exists, unified in this self-contained whole. Each contributes to the constitution of the whole and the whole is shared by every individual part.[1] Nous's importance within the Plotinian scheme is attributable to its status as the first instance of being and multiplicity.[2] In this respect, *Nous* provides the initial expression of otherness within the universe of being, maintaining the aloofness of this second hypostasis from the One. In this sense, *tolma* assumes a pivotal role in the emergence of *Nous*, providing what A.H. Armstrong has described as an "eternal standing away from that primal unity.[3] For, if anything other than the One is to exist, this ontological interval is essential. In effect, *tolma* insures the existence of something other than the One.

Plotinus's deliberations on the emergence of *Nous* proceed from a key question: how does a great number of things arise from one (πῶς οὖν ἑνὸς πλῆθος)?[4] Because the Plotinian One is a unified simplex, the very existence of multiplicity poses a major problem. The One is self-contained, admitting of neither magnitude nor quantity. Such spatial extension and numerical differentiation are earmarks of being, implying, in Plotinian terms, a dilution of power. As the source of being, the One cannot itself be included in the realm of being: the producer must exceed its products. This fact necessitates an absolutely unified source which demands no prior source. In keeping with the principles of Platonic philosophy, the One or the Good is posited above being, form, and definition.[5] Let us now consider some of the salient features of Plotinus's interpretation of the One and his understanding of its relationship to the hypostases of *Nous* and Soul.

The Role of the Plotinian One

In Plotinus's scheme, the One represents the ontological ground of the entire universe of being and the principle from which everything else is derived.[6] As absolutely transcendent, the One remains distinct from derivative being as the ultimate simplex which precedes being itself. While it differs from everything which follows after, it is capable of sharing its presence with the whole of reality. In this respect, it is interesting to note that Plotinus effected a decisive historical shift in the history of metaphysics by virtue of his characterization of the first principle as infinite, both in regard to its power and its very nature. This infinite character of the One is also based upon its pure unity: formless and incapable of numerical or quantitative measurement, it is completely free of any limitation. [7]

This interpretation of the first principle as wholly infinite made possible a more fully developed theory of participation, which overcame the deficiencies inherent in the Platonic theory, and its emphasis upon a static participation of individuals in universal concepts. In Plotinus, all lesser degrees of reality are totally dependent upon the One, not merely for their intelligibility, but for their very existence. Existence is ultimately derived from the One's boundless productivity. [8]

Plotinus continually resorted to metaphors and images in attempting to describe the One's emanation and its relationship to lower levels of reality. In *Ennead* III.8(30).10.3-10, the One is likened to a flowing spring of water which gives itself completely to its rivers and tributaries while remaining undiminished. In the same treatise, the creative outpouring is described in terms of the relationship between a plant and its root system, wherein life is transmitted without lessening the efficacy of the source in any way. Elsewhere, the One is compared to a fragrant substance whose aroma is diffused over a wide spatial area; as long as the substance remains, the fragrance persists. [9]

Such passages describe the One's transmission of life throughout the intelligible universe, a process which involves no corresponding weakening of the One's power. In this context, a key Plotinian metaphor is that of solar radiation: in various passages, the One is likened to the sun and emanation is described in terms of the diffusion of light.[10] Plato's influence upon Plotinus is apparent here, and the use of light imagery in the *Enneads* is highly reminiscent of its role in *Republic* VI (508-509) and VII (517-519). The solar metaphor is an extremely effective device in this context, emphasizing the One's absolute transcendence while allowing for its immanence to reality as a whole.

Because the One is both ontologically and conceptually transcendent, it is all but impossible to name or designate this principle in linguistic terms without compromising its nature. In its absolute simplicity, the One admits of no attributes. Plotinus viewed the appellation "One" as at least an adequate (or, the least inadequate) term, since it expresses the complete absence of plurality.[11] Plotinus thus defined the One in negative terms, and in this respect, he represents one of the chief exponents of the *via negativa* in the Western tradition. Again, the influence of Plato is apparent: Plotinus seems to adopt the terminology applied to the first hypostasis in the *Parmenides*, designating the One as infinite, unlimited, omnipresent, neither at rest nor in motion, timeless, indeterminate, indefinable, and unknow-able.[12]

The only major appellation which Plotinus imparts to the One is "Good," a name which he also inherited from Plato. In *Republic VI* (509b), Plato posited the Form of the Good above being itself, surpassing it in both dignity and power.[13] As in other instances, Plotinus used this name with reservation, stress-ing that it does not attempt to predicate goodness of the One, or for that matter, any other attribute associated with goodness. Rather, it merely serves his purposes as a means of identifica-tion without any affirmation of being.[14] Because "goodness" is so irreducible a concept, it alone can designate that which is fundamental to all things. But while the One or Good remains completely remote from being, being is inextricably bound up with this ultimate, originative Cause. [15]

The Tension

This consideration brings to the fore that troublesome tension inherent in Plotinus's emanation theory: implicit in the One's natural diffusiveness is a desire for otherness or a separate, autonomous existence. But to exist or to be other than the One implies imperfection on the part of that which estranges itself from its source. The problem is rooted in the fact that the One itself is ultimately the source of otherness and hence, the source of inferior, limited being. The desire to exist, however, is instrumental in the One's own diffusion. This tension is reflected in two disparate accounts used by Plotinus to explain the generation of plurality.

While the *Enneads* are rich in praise for the effects of the One's emanation, a negative attitude toward emanation emerges as well. From one standpoint, then, plurality is viewed in optimistic terms as the consequence of the One's own diffu-sion.[16] But a more pessimistic outlook attributes generation to an audacious act of *tolma*.[17] Philip Merlan succinctly defined the problem in these terms:

He has two alternatives: the 'falling away' from the One, and the over-flowing of the One. The presence of the two solutions which are mutu-ally exclusive reveals the difficulty . . . The passages explaining the origin of diversity by overflowing, i.e., as involuntary and necessary . . . are numerous and well-known. But the passages implying that the origin of diversity is some kind of 'falling away' are perhaps not always sufficiently stressed.[18]

Merlan's remarks point to an ambiguity in the *Enneads* regarding the generation of otherness by and from the One. This ambiguity is especially apparent in those passages wherein Plotinus describes *Nous* as desiring an independent existence. Such passages (*Enneads* VI.9(9).5.24-29; III.8(30).8.31-38; V.8(31).13.1-11) suggest a volition or choice on *Nous's* part for otherness which Plotinus views as both illegitimate and regrettable. In one particularly pointed passage, Plotinus asserts that it would have been better if *Nous* had never become second to the One (*Ennead* III.8(30).8.35-36). The problem stems from the fact that in order to generate at all, the One must produce something *other than itself*. However, that which is other than the One must be inferior and limited in relation to its source.

But if *Nous's* generation is blameworthy, then being, plurality, and ultimately, the material cosmos must be viewed in negative terms. A clarification of *tolma's* meaning on this primary level is crucial if one is to understand the nature of differentiation throughout the Plotinian universe. The tolmatic will to otherness underlying the emergence of *Nous* is subsequently manifested on the level of Soul, emerging in the generation of temporal process and in the descent of individual souls into material bodies.

It must be borne in mind, however, that the "difference" between the hypostases involves neither a spatial distance nor a temporal succession of any kind.[19] In this respect, it would be wrong to view *Nous* as *literally* "following after" the One, or Soul as "succeeding" *Nous* as the third hypostasis. Plotinus explicitly asserts that the order of the hypostases is based upon a relationship of subordination and dependence.[20] As Brehier has pointed out, the order is logical in nature; each hypostasis represents a different aspect of the One's outpouring.[21] Yet, each hypostasis is somehow distinct in its own eternal setting. Again, *tolma* assumes a vital role, maintaining this hypostatic differentiation throughout the entire scheme.

In actuality, Plotinus describes *Nous's* emergence in terms of two distinct phases. First, a desire for otherness manifests itself which proceeds from the One's own outpouring. This unformed desire is ultimately responsible for *Nous's* existence as a distinct hypostasis. At that moment, however, *Nous* is no more than an indeterminate potentiality, completely devoid of any intelligible content, constituting the raw substrate of multiplicity and otherness.[22]   Plotinus sometimes describes *Nous* in this unformed state in Aristotelian terms as "intelligible matter" (νοητή ὕλή) or the Indefinite *Dyad*. This *Dyad* serves as the pure potentiality for the further actualization of being.

Nous emerges as a distinct hypostasis only in the second phase or moment of Nous's emergence. Here, the indeterminate *Dyad*, that unformed desire for otherness receives form, definition, and intelligible content by virtue of its contemplation of the One.[23] When *Nous* contemplates the One, it transposes its primal unity into the multiplicity of intelligible Forms. Let us consider each of these phases in greater detail.

Differentiation and the *Dyad*

On its most basis level, *Nous's* differentiation from the One is explicable in numerical terms, as a movement from unity to plurality, from one to many: ". . . beginning as one (αρξάμενος ὡς ἕν) it did not remain as it began."[24] According to *Ennead* III.8(30).8.31-38, *Nous's* fault lies in its distention, when it becomes many. Because *Nous* is the intelligible principle of all things, it is not the intellect of one thing alone.[25]   Rather, it is universal in scope. Chapter nine of the same treatise elaborates on the manifold character of the second hypostasis: *Nous* cannot be the first because multiplicity comes after unity (i.e., in a logico-mathematical sense) and *Nous* is a number whose principle or cause is that which is unity (ὅτι πλῆθος ἐνὸς ὕστερον καὶ ἀριθμὸς δὲ οὗτος, ἀριθμοῦ δὲ ἀρχὴ καὶ του τοιούτου τὸ ὄντως ἕν'').[26]

Nous's derivative nature is reflected in its designation as the "*Dyad*." This "dyadic" aspect of *Nous* has been analyzed in several   detailed scholarly works, from a number of standpoints.[27] A consideration of the more salient features of Plotinus's treatment of this topic will suffice for the present purposes. *Ennead* V.l(10).5.13-17 refers the appellations "number" and "*Dyad*" to the intelligible principles and to *Nous* respectively. Plotinus goes on to assert that the *Dyad* is indeterminate, providing the underlying substrate of the intelligible world.[28] The *Dyad* represents *Nous* in its primal state, manifesting itself as a desire for otherness. The emergence of the *Dyad* coincides with the emergence of plurality. But what emerges is a formless potentiality—indeterminate, like the power of vision, or in MacKenna's translation, "a vague readiness for any and every vision." At this level, *Nous* is merely intelligible matter, the unformed substrate of differentiation.

In *Ennead* II.4(12).5.29-31, Plotinus asserts that otherness and movement provide the co-principles of this intelligible matter: movement produces otherness and otherness is bound up with movement. Both principles remain undefined and need the One for formation and definition. Metaphorically, the One illuminates the "darkness" of matter. By turning toward the One in contemplation, the substrate becomes *Nous*, the Intellectual-Principle and the world of true being. [29]

This primary phase of *Nous's* emergence must be understood within the context of Neopythagorean philosophy. In Neopythagorean terms, the *Dyad* was the principle of multiplicity, and by implication, of evil. Ample scholarly evidence exists to support the contention that various members of the Neopythagorean school of Middle Platonism called the *Dyad* "*tolma*."[30] By associating the *Dyad* with *tolma*, primal differentiation was equated with evil, deficiency, and non-being. The *Dyad* also assumed a dynamic character as an audacious drive toward otherness. Conversely, *tolma* became the principle responsible for the very emergence of otherness.

To what degree did Plotinus equate the *Dyad* with *tolma*? Unlike his Neopythagorean predecessors and contemporaries, he never explicitly referred to the *Dyad* in this manner. But it is likely that Plotinus was at least aware of the traditional association of the two terms. For, by the third century, A.D., the *Dyad* had acquired an unmistakable Neopythagorean character, along with the attendant belief that the emergence of plurality is an evil. By calling *Nous* the "*Dyad*" (*Ennead* V.l(10).5.13-17), Plotinus

made a statement whose import reveals itself against this
Neopythagorean background: the very foundation of *Nous*, the
first instance of being and plurality, lies in a tolmatic desire to
be other than the One. In this respect, *tolma* provides the
dynamic element implicit in *Nous's* severance from the One.[31]
An appreciation of the conceptual merger of the *Dyad* and *tolma*
is thus extremely important in approaching Plotinus's discussion of primal differentiation.

Nous's Contemplation of the One

As we saw above, the intelligible matter which proceeds from
the One is indeterminate and purely derivative in character.
Determination occurs only in the second phase of *Nous's* generation, where the dyadic substrate becomes the Intellectual-Principle, by virtue of its contemplation of the One.[32] Just as *tolma*
is instrumental in the *Dyad's* initial emergence, it is also present
in its contemplative vision of the One, the act whereby it
becomes the full-fledged hypostasis.

Strictly speaking, there are no separate phases or moments in
Nous's emergence as a distinct hypostasis. Yet, Plotinus clearly
writes as if *Nous* proceeds in a series of successive stages, from
unformed *Dyad*, to contemplator of the One, to *Nous*—the intelligible world of Forms. We might interpret these phases as
different aspects of the same movement toward primal differentiation, just as we interpret the hypostases of *Nous* and Soul as
separate aspects of the One's productive power. While *tolma* is
operative in the initial separation of the *Dyad*, it also appears to
be necessary in maintaining that separation once *Nous* is fully
informed by the One.

The intellective act whereby *Nous* becomes informed and
defined by the One results in the establishment of being. The
act is described metaphorically, in terms of visual experience:
like the eyes, the *Dyad* has the potential for vision, as a sight not
yet seeing (ὡς ὄψις οὕτω ἰδοῦσα). This raw potential for
intellection is actualized once the *Dyad* directs its gaze toward
the One, a "seeing" whereby a similitude is achieved between
the knower and its object. A strong mystical element manifests
itself in Plotinus's description of this contemplative vision.[33]

The One constitutes the ultimate Good, the highest perfection toward which any knower can aspire. The *Dyad* experiences a kind of premonition or presentiment (φάντασμα) of the One's primal unity which prompts an inclination or propensity (ἔφεσις) to become identical with the One. [34]

Ennead III.8(30).8.11 provides an extended statement regarding this rather complex movement. Once again, Plotinus resorts to a visual analogue, this time reinforcing it with Aristotelian terminology. For the present purposes, a summary of this rich passage will suffice. Plotinus first likens *Nous* to an eye which is in the act of seeing; as such, it was formerly a potentiality which has now been actualized. It is the Good which brings *Nous's* vision to its fullness. For, when *Nous* confronts the Good, it becomes analogous to it and thereby, Nous is brought to completion. By virtue of this conformance, the Good imposes Form upon *Nous*, which bears its imprint and encompasses the nature of being within itself. Figuratively, *Nous* is the "offspring" of the Good, like a beautiful child filled with its fullness. [35]

Even in its indeterminate state, the *Dyad* assumes a special dignity, insofar as it directs itself to the highest possible object of intellection. But the *Dyad* cannot receive the One in its pure simplicity: because the *Dyad* is already a manifold (albeit an unformed one), it receives the One as a manifold. In this respect, the *Dyad* functions like a filter through which the One's boundless power becomes variegated. The *Dyad* "sees" the One as the world of intelligible Forms. In effect, the object of intellection (i.e., the One) is the cause of *Nous* as Intelligible-Principle. *Nous* comes into its own only when it receives determination by the One. But, in a sense, *Nous* also determines itself through its vision of the One.

In classic Hellenic terms, being implies form, limitation, and determination. Since the One transcends being, it also transcends the Forms. *Nous* "translates" the sheer power of the One into the Forms, the intelligible paradigms of all things which provide *Nous's* content.[36] Since intellection necessarily involves a duality between a knower and that which is known, the One cannot be grasped as it is in itself, precisely because it defies all conceptualization and any attempt at objectification. [37]

If *Nous* is to function as the Intellectual-Principle, the repository of Forms, it must remain distinct from the One. Accordingly, its natural gravitation must be held in check. *Nous* is never
subsumed by the Good, but remains just "near" enough to
receive the full impact of its forming power. Does it not appear,
however, than an act of *tolma* is implicit in the maintenance of
this ontological separation or, as Armstrong describes it, an
"eternal standing away?"[38] It seems that an element of *tolma*
must be presupposed if *Nous* is to remain distinct from the One.
In the absence of such a will to otherness, *Nous* would follow its
inborn propensity to return to the Good, becoming reabsorbed
by the very unity which it so passionately desires. *Nous* thus
moves toward a reunification with its source which cannot be
consummated.

Nous's Voluntarism

Although the One is unified and self-contained, it continually
diffuses itself in the emanation of being. But Plotinus distinguishes between the One and the movement which it initiates.[39]
The paradox lies in the fact that the One is the source of a
movement which it does not itself possess. In effect, the One
gives rise to the primal differentiation which underlies *Nous* as
the second hypostasis. In this sense, *tolma* assumes the proportions of a metaphysical principle in its own right, ultimately
derived from the One, yet treated as a separate element. As
Baladi points out, the vast ontological gulf between the One and
its effects cannot be bridged by means of emanation alone: a
secondary principle is needed which will provide for the procession of being, plurality, and otherness while insuring that differentiation will be sustained.[40] *Tolma*, the will to otherness,
serves as this principle of otherness and differentiation.

In several passages, Plotinus suggests that *Nous* acts on its
own account, opting for a mode of existence apart from the
One (*Enneads* V.1(10).7.13-17; VI.9(9).5.24-29; III.8(30).8.31-38;
V.8(31).13.1-11). In this respect, *Nous* seems to operate as a co-
principle of the One.[41] The language suggests that *Nous* somehow existed prior to its actual generation. Because *Nous*
depends upon the One for its being, however, this is not possi-

ble. Nevertheless, Plotinus depicts *Nous* as opting for separate existence and autonomy. The implication seems to be that *Nous* existed in a seminal condition even prior to its outward procession.

Such sentiments are apparent in *Ennead* VI.9(9).5.24-29, a passage which explicitly uses the verb-form "τολμήσας" in connection with *Nous's* estrangement from the One. Plotinus describes *Nous's* unique relationship to the first principle and its almost inexplicable desire to exist apart from its source.

> Now that which is before what is most honored among beings, if indeed it is necessary that there is before Nous that which is desiring to be one but is not one but in the form of oneness, because Nous is not spread about in itself, but is really united in itself, not dividing itself by virtue of its nearness next after the One, but somehow it desired to stand apart from the One with audacity (εαυτὸν τῷ πλησίον μετὰ το ῾ἐν εἶναι ἀποστῆναι δέ πως τοῦ ἑνὸς τολμήσας) . . . [42]

The phrase which demands further analysis is "ἀποστῆναι δέ πως ἑνὸς τολμήσας." "τολμήσας," the verb-form of the substantive *tolma*, designates an audacious desire to be or to exist independently of the One. But what is the consequence of this audacious desire for autonomy? The answer is provided by the infinitive *"apostanai"* (ἀποστῆναι) related to the verb-form *"aphistomai"* (αφίστομαι), whose primary meaning is "to make revolt."[43] In a political context, the term connotes a whole cluster of meanings: to upset an established order, to cause internal upheaval, to usurp a higher authority. All of these sentiments are implicit in *Nous's* movement from the One. *Ennead* VI.9(9).5.24-29 suggests a deviation, withdrawal, or schism of a lower from a higher principle.

But "ἀποστῆναι" also possesses another key meaning which is applicable to *Nous* in its movement from the One: *Nous* wills "to stand apart" from its source. It is this "standing apart" or withdrawal which constitutes a culpable act. The reason for this movement remains a puzzle for Plotinus, and his use of "πως" underscores his uncertainty. He asserts that *Nous* "*somehow*" dared to stand apart, as if the motive were obscure. Indeed, how could anything desire to exist apart from the One? Yet, *Nous* opts for otherness. One finds, as Merlan observed, an implication of voluntarism in both *tolma* and *apostanai*. [44]

In addition to *Ennead* VI.9(9).5.24-29, two other passages stress *Nous's* willingness to stand apart from the One. *Nous* is depicted as acting on its own initiative in both *Enneads* V.8(31).13.1-11 and III.8(30).8.31-38. In *Ennead* V.8(31).13.1-11, Plotinus's account of *Nous's* severance from the One is flavored with mythological imagery. *Nous*, symbolized by *Kronos*, holds a middle-ground between the One (symbolized by *Ouranos*) and Soul (symbolized by *Zeus*, and alternately, *Aphrodite*).

> Thus, the god who is bound so that he remains the same and has given over the rule of all things to the son—for it was not to his taste to relinquish his rule and to pursue the one . . . coming afterward, having a satiety with its beauties—he relinquishes this and appoints his father in himself . . . and on the other side appoints that which begins with the son after himself, so that between the two he becomes by the otherness of his secession from what is on high and by the bond holding him from what is after him (ὥστε μεταξὺ ἀμφοῖν γενέσθαι τῇ τε ἑτερότητι τῆς πρὸς τὸ ᾽άνω ἀποτομῆς καὶ τῷ ἀνέχοντι ἀπὸ τοῦ μετ᾽ αὐτὸν), being between a superior father and an inferior son. [45]

In *Ennead* III.8(30).8.31-38, one also finds a clear emphasis upon voluntarism:

> But beginning as one it did not stay as it began (ἀρξάμενας ὡς ἐν οὐχ ὡς ἤρξατο ἔμεινεν), but became many (πολὺς γενόμενος) as if heavy (οἷον βεβαρημένος), and unrolled itself (καὶ ἐξείλιξεν αὐτὸν) because it wanted to possess everything (παντα᾽έχειν θέλων). [46]

Here, *Nous's* audacity is rooted in a desire to over-extend itself, wishing "to possess all things." Plotinus employs the metaphor of a circle "unravelling itself" (οἷον γὰρ κύκλος ἐξελίξας αὐτὸν) to describe this expansive movement.[47] Self-assertion leads to a fragmentation and dilution of power. The passage further suggests a slothfulness and moral laxity on *Nous's* part.[48]

Interestingly, *Enneads* III.8(30) and V.8(31) represent two of Plotinus's "anti-Gnostic" polemics (along with *Enneads* V.5(32) and II.9(33)). In spite of this, Plotinus seems to resort to the motifs and language of the very sects which he opposes. Whatever the reasons for *Nous's* exodus, *Ennead* III.8(30).8.31-38 is clearly pessimistic in tone. The will toward otherness is viewed as a blameworthy act. *Nous's* desire to possess all things is wrong because it opens the way for the emergence of the manifold. While neither *Enneads* III.8(30).8.31-38 nor V.8(31).13.1-11 resort to the use of *tolma*-language, an element of arrogance is implied in this movement from the One that hints at a tolmatic spirit. The passages suggest the presence of a restless, turbulent nature which is the very antithesis of the life of rest, unity, and self-containedness that characterizes the One. *Nous's* error lies in its boldness to exist apart from this supremely perfect principle.

Diverse Scholarly Interpretations

Two distinct lines of scholarship have emerged regarding the intepretation of *tolma* on the level of *Nous*. Armstrong's remarks express the sum and substance of the more dominant interpretation:

> . . . the idea . . . appears in a few passages . . . that the original giving-out of the indeterminate vitality, the 'indefinite dyad' which is the basis of Intellect, from the One, and the giving-out of Soul from Intellect which is the next stage in the 'unfolding' of derived being and depends upon the first, are acts of illegitimate self-assertion (τόλμα). All existence, in this way of looking at it, depends on a kind of radical original sin, a wish for separation and independence . . . a desire directed away from the One, a desire which produces . . . otherness. [49]

Armstrong's remarks highlight the paradoxical character of *Nous's* detachment from the One. On the one hand, generation is determined; on the other hand, it is voluntary. The One produces a desire to be other than itself. This desire is the basis of *Nous's tolma*, bespeaking a latent element of the irrational in an otherwise highly rationalistic metaphysical scheme. This view is consistent with that of Philip Merlan, who, as we have observed, characterized Plotinian emanation theory as an alliance of an optimistic account (stressing the One's diffusiveness) and a pessimistic account that depicts the processional movement in terms of a "fall" or descent. [50]

A challenge to this viewpoint is posed by John Rist. While he directs his remarks to *Ennead* VI.9(9).5.24-29, they have relevance for any consideration of *Nous's tolma*. Rist contends that *Nous's* "standing apart" from the One lacks any element of voluntariness whatsoever. Rather, he maintains that *Nous* proceeds as a consequence of the One's "generosity" or natural self-diffusiveness.

> The question with which we are concerned at 6.9.5.29 is whether the first generated thing—intelligible matter—came into being because of τόλμα. In other words, how do we interpret the word τολμήσας in view of the fact that ἀποστῆναι means to "stand apart"? We should notice at once that the passage does not in fact concern the generation of *Nous* (its "coming to stand apart") but rather its attitude after it has been generated (its actual "standing apart"). Thus the fact that *Nous* "dared" ἀποστῆναι τοῦ ἑνός does not mean that it recklessly broke away, but that it has "faced up" to living apart after its generation—indeed it had no option. This lack of option and the consequent τόλμα of *Nous* is not a guilty act on *Nous's* part, which brought about its own fall, but is rather the inevitable result of the One's generosity. [51]

Rist bases his argument upon an interpretation of the phrase "ἀποστῆναι δέ πως ἑνὸς τολμήσας," approaching the text in terms of *Nous's* attitude only after it has been generated by the One. But he completely bypasses the crucial issue regarding the tension between the optimistic and pessimistic attitudes toward otherness that one finds in the *Enneads*. According to Rist's interpretation, τολμήσας implies no more than a kind of stoical resignation to its fate to be other than the One. This interpretation, I believe, is problematical for a number of reasons.

To begin with, a reading of Plotinus clearly discloses two distinct strains of thought regarding the emergence of plurality. On the one hand, Plotinus views plurality as the necessary implication of the One's own emanation and diffusion. From this standpoint, plurality is good because it proceeds from an absolutely perfect source. On the other hand, however, Plotinus views the very emergence of plurality as somehow wrong. From this pessimistic standpoint, plurality is the consequence of a fall, prompted by an illegitimate act of self-assertion. Various texts (see Chapter V, below) provide ample evidence of such a pessimistic strain in Plotinian thinking. If taken in isolation, Rist's remarks might lead one to believe that no such tension emerges in the *Enneads*.

Secondly, it really seems irrelevant whether the phrase "ἀποστῆναι δέ πως ἑνὸς τολμήσας" refers to (1) *Nous's* "coming to stand apart" or to (2) *Nous's* "actual standing apart" once it has been generated by the One. Rist opts for the second interpretation alone. But in either case, *Nous* must exhibit a desire or *tolma* to be other than the One. In this respect, however, *Nous's tolma* actually assumes a dual role. At the outset, *tolma* initiates *Nous's* "standing apart" which constitutes an audacious drive toward otherness. Support for this contention is found in those Plotinian passages which stress a voluntarism on *Nous's* part: *Enneads* VI.9(9).5.24-29, III.8(30).8.31-38, and V.8(31).13.1-11 all suggest a voluntary movement toward otherness and differentiation. They show that *Nous wills* "to stand apart" from the One. (Rist, in fact, concedes that *Ennead* VI.9(9).5.24-29 contains an "echo" of the Neopythagorean conception of *tolma*.52) But it can be argued that even after its emergence, *Nous* requires an act of *tolma* to sustain it as a distinct hypostasis. In the absence of such an "aloofness," nothing other than the One could exist. *Nous's* very being is thus contingent upon a desire for autonomy which contains an element of audacity.

Rist's contention that *Nous* had no option but to remain apart from the One is a valid one. However, he seems to downplay the importance of *tolma* in prompting this "standing away" or "standing apart." In Plotinian terms, the One is the supreme Good, the best of all objects. The "will to otherness" which accounts for the emergence of plurality is complemented by a desire for unification with the One at all levels of the Plotinian universe. In the absence of *tolma*, or some such principle of differentiation, *Nous* (as well as everything else) would be subsumed by the One.

Plotinus's metaphysical scheme thus requires a principle of differentiation which allows *Nous* to exist as eternal contemplator of the One. Armstrong's most recent comments on this topic are most enlightening:

> It is the Good which produces the unformed life which in its contemplative return becomes the best being there can be...but the return must be eternally checked if anything other than the Good is to exist at all; Intellect, the World of creative Forms, cannot ever simply disappear back into the primal unity if the Good is to diffuse himself as he must. It is this checked return, this eternal "standing away," this separation which leaves Intellect as near the One as is compatible with separate existence, which is the primary τόλμα on which any audacities which may be discerned at lower levels ultimately depend. [53]

In response to Rist, then, one finds an apparent fault-line in Plotinus's deliberations on the procession of being from the One. Rather than relying solely upon an optimistic emanation/ diffusion account, Plotinus also develops a pessimistic account which reflects a lingering dependence upon Gnostic and Neopythagorean ideas. *Tolma* is instrumental in the outward procession of *Nous*, the first instance of plurality. One finds evidence that Plotinus viewed *tolma* as responsible for *Nous's* "standing apart" in those texts which suggest that *Nous* voluntarily secedes from its primal source (i.e., *Enneads* VI.9(9).5.24-29; V.8(31).13.1-11; III.8(30).8.31-38). But one can also argue that *tolma* (as a will toward separate existence) is responsible for sustaining *Nous* once it has "stood apart" from the One. In effect, *tolma* insures *Nous's* continued existence as a distinct hypostasis.

Summation

I have argued that *tolma* is constitutive of *Nous* as a distinct hypostasis, that is, instrumental in its very emergence. The existence of the Intellectual-Principle is grounded upon a desire for otherness. This desire assumes two forms: (1) the initial *tolma* toward separate existence; and (2) the *tolma* sustaining otherness, the enduring will to remain distinct from the One. The first expression of *tolma* functions as a dynamic element in the *Dyad's* separation from the One. The second expression of *tolma* serves as a principle of stabilization, fixing *Nous* in place, so to speak, as recipient of the One's formative power.

Tolma, it would appear, must be viewed as implicit in both of these moments of *Nous's* generation, manifesting itself in the will toward otherness which proceeds from the One, while sustaining *Nous's* otherness or existence apart from the One. Such otherness is necessary if *Nous* is to endure as the second hypostasis, the repository of intelligible Forms and the first instance of being. In effect, *tolma* (or some such principle of differentiation) sustains *Nous* in perpetuity, maintaining the crucial "distance" from the One which permits it to engage in its eternal contemplation of its source. In the absence of *tolma*, *Nous* would follow the natural inclination of all things to return to the One, the *Summum Bonum* of all reality. Because of this "sustained aloofness," the *tolma* of *Nous* is at least indirectly responsible for the establishment of being by making the existence of something other than the One possible.

Plotinus's discussions concerning the emergence of *Nous* provide the basis of a tension which permeates the entire intelligible universe. The conflict between an optimistic emanation/ diffusion account and pessimistic fall accounts also manifests itself on the level of Soul. *Tolma* assumes a crucial role in these psychological accounts. I next turn to an examination of Plotinus's psychological theory as a prelude to my investigation of the various expressions of *tolma* in the third hypostasis.

Notes

1. *Ennead* VI.2(43).22.10-13.
   cf. *Enneads* V.9(5).6.7-9; V.7(38).17.25-27; I.8(51).2.15-21.

2. *Enneads* V.6(24).5.5-10.
   cf. V.2(11).1.7-13.
   A.H. Armstrong conveniently enumerates *Nous's* various roles within the Plotinian scheme (*The Architecture of the Intelligible Universe in the Philosophy of Plotinus*, Cambridge, 1940, pp. 49-50): "Its different aspects may be summarily classified as follows: (i) it is a radiation, or efflux from the One, like light from the sun. (ii) In a few passages it is conceived as the first unfolding of the potentialities of the One, which is a seed holding all things in potency. (iii) It is the highest phase of Intellect, both human and universal, which directly contemplating the One apprehends it in the idea that *Nous* proceeds from the One as a potency and is actualized by returning upon it in contemplation. (v) It is the Intellectual Cosmos, a world organism which contains the archetypes of all things in the visible universe. As such it possesses to the full that organic unity which the later, "Posidonian" Stoics had predicated of the visible, for them, the only, cosmos, but which Plotinus had denied to it any full or real sense. (vi) This aspect is to some extent connected with the psychological side of *Nous* by considering it as a universe of interpenetrating spiritual beings each containing all the others organically united to its contemplation."

3. A.H. Armstrong, "Gnosis and Greek Philosophy," in *Gnosis* (Festschrift für Hans Jonas, Göttingen, 1978), p. 118.

4. *Ennead* III.9(13).4.1.

5. *Ennead*   V.4(7).1.5-15; VI.9(9).5.29-42; V.2(11).1.1-7; VI.4(22).9.24-25; V.6(24).3.21-24; V.5(32).11.4-11; VI.7(38).17.6-14;32.5-14; V.3(49).16.13-16.

6. *Ennead* V.4(7).1.34-41.

7. *Ennead* V.5(32).11.4-11.

8. *Ennead* V.5(32).10.10-14.

9. *Ennead* V.1(10).6.30-39.

10. *Ennead* V.3(49).12.39-44; cf. *Enneads* V.3(49).17.33-37; I.7(54).1.24-28; VI.4(22).7.38-42.

11. *Ennead* V.5(32).6.11-37.

12. E. R. Dodds first recognized the influence of the *Parmenides* upon Plotinus in his landmark article "The Parmenides of Plato and the Origin of the Neoplatonic One," *Classical Quarterly* 22 (1928): 129-142. Dodds established parallels between certain key passages in the *Parmenides* (137D-E; 138A; 139B; 139E; 140B; 141A; 141E; 142A; 144B; 145A-B; 145E; 146A) and Plotinus's language about the One.
    cf. *Ennead* V.5(32).ll.1-5; V.5(32).9.33-38; VI.9(9).3.37-45; V.5(32).6.1-37; V.5(32).4.6-18.

13. Plato, *Republic* VI, 509b, trans. F. M. Cornford (Oxford, 1950): ". . . and Goodness is not the same thing as being, but even beyond being, surpassing it in dignity and power."

14. *Ennead* VI.7(38).38.1-4.

15. *Ennead* V.3(49).12.33-38.

16. *Ennead* VI.7(38).18.41-51. cf. *Ennead* V.1(10).7.1-6.

17. For *Nous*, as we have seen, the relevant passages are *Enneads* VI.9(9).5.24-29; III.8(30).8.31-38; V.8(31).13.1-11.

18. Philip Merlan, *From Platonism to Neoplatonism* (The Hague: Martinus Nijhoff, 1960), p. 124.

19. *Ennead* VI.4(22).4.18-26. cf. *Ennead* VI.4(22).11.1-10.

20. *Ennead* V.1(10).6.16-25; VI.4(22).14.5-14.

21. Emile Brehier, *The Philosophy of Plotinus*, trans. Joseph Thomas (Chicago: University of Chicago Press, 1971), p. 47: "It follows that the development according to which a hypostasis arises from another has a permanent, fixed, and eternal character. The succession in which we consider the hypostases is . . . a logical order."

22. *Ennead* II.4(12).5.1-5; V.1(10).5.6-19; V.4(7).2.4-10; V.3(49).11.1-12; VI.7(38).16.13-24;17.1-9.

23. *Ennead* II.4(12).5.31-39; V.1(10).5.6-9; V.3(49).11.11-16; VI.7(38).15.10-17; V.2(11).1.9-16.

24. *Ennead* III.8(30).8.32-33.

25. *Ennead* III.8(30).8.40-42; cf. *Ennead* II.4(12).3.9-17.

26. *Ennead* III.8(30).9.3-4.

27. A. H. Armstrong, *The Architecture of the Intelligible Universe in the Philosophy of Plotinus* (Cambridge, 1940), pp. 65-81; "Spiritual or Intelligible Matter in Plotinus and St. Augustine," *Augustinus Magister* I (Paris, 1965): 277-283; *The Cambridge History of Later Greek and Early Medieval Philosophy* (Cambridge, 1970), pp. 241-249. Also see John M. Rist, "The Indefinite *Dyad* and Intelligible Matter in Plotinus," *Classical Quarterly* (New Series) 12 (1962): 99-107; "Monism: Plotinus and Some Predecessors," *Harvard Studies in Classical Philology* 70 (1965): 338.

28. *Ennead* V.1(10).5.13-19.

29. *Ennead* II.4(12).5.31-39.
    A. H. Armstrong (*The Architecture of the Intelligible Universe in the Philosophy of Plotinus*, p. 67) provides an insightful commentary on this key passage: "He . . . gives an account of the origin of matter in the intelligible world according to which it is eternally generated from the First, produced by 'otherness' which is 'the first movement.' This 'movement' or 'otherness,' the outgoing of Nous from the One, is αόριστος until it returns upon the One and is informed or delimited . . . by it. It is itself dark but is illuminated by the First, which is other than it. Here we have obviously returned from Aristotle to Plato; much of the language which Plotinus uses is clearly derived direct from the *Sophist* or the *Philebus*." cf. III.8(30).11.15-26.

30. The evidence is summarized by John M. Rist, "Monism: Plotinus and Some Predecessors," p. 338.

31. Rist, "Monism: Plotinus and Some Predecessors," p. 341: ". . . we may wonder if there is not a further echo of the Pythagorean conception in 6.9.5.29, where *Nous* is said to have 'dared' (τολμήσας) in some way to stand apart (ἀποστῆναι) from the One."

32. *Ennead* V.1(10).7.1-6.   cf.   *Enneads* V.1(10).5.6-9;   II.4(12).4.4-11; V.2(11).1.7-13.

33. *Ennead* V.3(49).11.4-5.

34. *Ennead* III.8(30).11.15-29.

35. *Ennead* III.8(30).11.1-2;33-35. cf. *Ennead* V.1(10).5.18-19; V.6(24).5.5-10.

36. *Ennead* III.8(30).8.26-32; VI.7(38).15.14-20;V.3(49).11. 1-11.
    Plotinus's deliberations on *Nous's* contemplative vision of the One are charged with a powerful mystical quality. But they also call to mind the Aristotelian dictum that the knower becomes identical with that which is known by virtue of the intellective act.
    cf. Aristotle, *Metaphysics* 1027b21; *De Anima* 430a19.

37. *Ennead* V.3(49).11.12-30; V.3(49).10.46-51.

38. A. H. Armstrong, "Gnosis and Greek Philosophy," p. 118.

39. *Enneads* V.5(32).10.10-18; III.2(47).4.13-16; VI.9(9).3. 39-45; II.4(12).5.30-34; V.1(10).6.19-27; VI.8(39).8.8-14.

40. Naguib Baladi, "Origine et Signification de l'Audace chez Plotin," *Le Néoplatonisme* (Royaumant, 1971), p. 89: "Entre l'Un et les autres hypostheses, en deça de l'Un et aux différents niveaux de l'etre, entre l'etre divin et l'etre sensible, il y a un rapport originel qui prime celui de la procession et al procession et de l'émanation, d'une procession qui est émanation. Le surgissement de l'être, la multiplicité propre a l'être intelligible, la variété infinie et infiniment concrete de ses manifestations (V, 8, 4; 8, 9-10; VI, 7, 12), la dualite irreductible de l'intelligence et de l'intelligible, l'apparition du sensible, l'union de l'âme au corps, le mal comme la mort, tout cela ne saurait être compris ni expliqué dans un système d'émanation pure, et en vertu de la simple position de l'Un, de la profusion et de la surabondance de sa puissance. Ce sont là certes des conséquences qui peuvent être rattachées directement à l'Un et a sa toute-puissance, mais qui presupposent, un peupartout des fissures ou des eclatements, tout au moins une altérité et des différences irréductibles. -Si, l'Un est principe premier et absolu, l'avènement de ces effets requiert comme un principe second qui fait que l'être surgit et que l'altérité prend droit a l'être. Ce principe de surgissement et finalement et séparation, est l'audace même."

41. *Ennead* V.1(10).7.27-32.
cf. A. H. Armstrong, "Gnosis and Greek Philosophy," p. 118: ". . . in Neoplatonic thought every created or derived being is co-responsible for its own creation or deviation . . ."

42. cf. Brehier's translation: "Il est antérieur à celui des êtres qui a la valeur la plus haute, parce qu'il y a a nécessairement un terme antérieur à l'Intelligence; celle-ci veut être mais semblable a l'Un; elle ne se disperse pas, et elle reste véritablement avec elle-même parce qu'elle voisine de l'Un et qu'elle vient après lui; mais elle a eu l'audace de s'écarter de lui."

43. Liddell and Scott, *Greek-English Lexicon* (Oxford, 1977), p. 120. cf. *apostasis* (ἀποστασις), i.e., "standing away," defection or revolt, departure or removal from, a distance or interval of some kind (*Liddell and Scott*, p. 93).

44. Philip Merlan, *From Platonism to Neoplatonism*, p. 124.

45. *Ennead* V.8(31).13.1-11.

46. *Ennead* III.8(30).8.32-34.

47. *Ennead* III.8(30).8.36.

48. Armstrong translates the phrase "οἶον βεβαρημένος" as a "heaviness due to drunken sleep." The language resembles what we encounter in Origen's fall account in the *De Principiis* (II,8,3), where rational natures are said to grow "sated" with the Divine love and the contemplation of the Divine nature (κόρον δε αὐτὰς λαβεῖν τῆς θείας ἀγάπης καὶ θεωριας . . .)

49. A. H. Armstrong, *The Cambridge History of Later Greek and Early Medieval Philosophy*, p. 242.

50. The relevant passages for the pessimistic account are found in *Ennead* VI.9(9).5.24-29; V.8(31).13.1-11; and III.8(30).8.31-38.

51. John M. Rist, "Monism: Plotinus and Some Predecessors," pp. 341-342.

52. See note #31, above.

53. A. H. Armstrong, "Gnosis and Greek Philosophy," pp. 117-118.

Chapter III

The Nature and Varieties of Soul
in Plotinus

Soul, the third hypostasis in Plotinus's metaphysical scheme, is derived from *Nous*, which provides it with form and intelligibility (*Ennead* II.3(52).17.15-18). Just as the One precedes and vivifies *Nous*, *Nous* precedes and vivifies Soul. In this respect, *Nous* is designated as the "Form of the Soul." Soul occupies the crucial middle-ground between the noetic and the material orders. In MacKenna's rendering, it assumes a "mid-rank" position: Soul has a kind of "amphibious" character, possessing a divine nature while bordering on the periphery of the sense world and acting as its spiritual and rational principle. [1]

Both *Nous* and Soul are closely aligned within the Plotinian scheme. In several passages, Plotinus affirms this kinship, characterizing Soul as the very image of *Nous*. Soul is informed by *Nous* and shares in its contemplation of the One. *Nous* and the totality of souls constitute the intellectual cosmos, the locus of real essences. Soul, however, has a dual focus: while its highest phase retains this close association with *Nous*, a lower phase is oriented toward the material cosmos. This lower phase, the World Soul, becomes time-bound as the result of a desire for self-determination. Such a desire is instrumental in effecting the transition between the eternal and temporal orders (*Ennead* III.7(45).ll.15-20). This transition involves a declination from the self-contained life of eternal contemplation to one of process, change, and activity. [2]

But, at the outset, it must be stressed that the topic of the third hypostasis represents one of the most complicated aspects of Plotinian metaphysics, and Plotinus frequently displays inconsistencies in this area of his thinking. Accordingly, we must consider Plotinus's views regarding the nature and varieties of Soul before analyzing the role of *tolma* on this level.

Three different levels of Soul are discussed in the *Enneads*: All-Soul or Soul-Entire; World-Soul or Cosmic Soul; and individual souls. The problem is only compounded in the face of Plotinus's affirmation that all souls are one.[3] In spite of this affirmation of the unicity of Soul, the above-mentioned levels are often treated on a separate basis. Let us temporarily bypass the critical issue of their relationship and examine the activities of each level of Soul.

All-Soul or Soul-Entire is the totality of spiritual life, an all-inclusive, all-encompassing principle. It is literally all things, not confined to any particular reality. Rather, the universe of things is contained in and embraced by Soul.[4] The World Soul is specifically concerned with the material cosmos. Its activity involves the governance of Nature and physical bodies; it thereby assumes a "downward" focus that directs its gaze away from the intelligible realities contained in Nous. Indeed, this constitutes one of the distinguishing characteristics of Soul, for if it were only engaged in intellection and contemplation, it would be wholly indistinguishable from *Nous* (*Ennead* IV.8(6).3.21-25). But as a principle of intelligibility and spirituality in its own right, it actively communicates form to the lower world. Accordingly, Plotinus views the material cosmos as a beautiful creation, precisely because it is the manifestation of the divine.[5]

The Unicity and Omnipresence of Soul

Plotinus maintains that the hypostasis Soul is a unified whole, containing within itself the totality of souls (i.e., the World Soul and individual souls). An implication of this teaching is that all souls are ultimately one. But, for the purposes of this study, that teaching poses two key problems. First, it might be questioned whether *tolma* initiates a fragmentation of the hypostasis Soul into its lower phases. If this be the case, then the World Soul and individual souls might be mere "offshoots" of a higher psychological principle. Secondly, the affirmation of Soul's unicity calls into question the individuality of souls: if all souls are one, can "individual" souls truly exist? A preliminary clarification of these issues is necessary before proceeding to an analysis of *tolma* on the level of Soul.

In *Ennead* IV.9(8), Plotinus principally addresses the question as to whether all souls are one. This treatise provides the clearest statement in the *Enneads* regarding the unicity of Soul. Plotinus begins by affirming the omnipresence of Soul throughout the individual body: Soul is not confined to one portion of the individual but permeates the whole being. The unity of human beings is thus derived from the unity of the individual soul. But this unity on an individual level is traceable to a higher principle: "if my soul and your soul are from the Soul of the All and that Soul is one, it is necessary that these souls are one also" (εἰ μὲν οὖν ἐκ τῆς τοῦ παντὸς καὶ ἡ ἐμὴ καὶ ἡ σή, μιὰ δὲ ἐκείνη, καὶ ταύτας δεῖ εἶναι μίαν). Moreover, Plotinus contends that if the Soul of the All and my soul are derived from one soul, again all souls are one (Εἰ δὲ καὶ ἡ τοῦ παντὸς καὶ ἡ εμὴ ἐκ ψυχῆς μιᾶς, πάλιν αὖ πᾶσαι μία).[6]

Plotinus himself recognized the difficulties inherent in such a theory, since it might well imply that individual experiences are universally shared. However, the alternative is clear. If the unicity of Soul is denied, then the universe ceases to be unified and individual souls lose their mutual bond. But if only one Soul exists, how do we account for individual differences and subjective experiences? Plotinus addresses this question in the second chapter of the treatise, maintaining that the doctrine of Soul's unity does not demand that all souls be identical. Instead, the recipient body is the controlling factor, for an identical thing in different recipients will have different experiences.

Plotinus does not wish to uphold Soul's unicity at the expense of individuality. Rather, he argues that Soul is simultaneously one and many: it is a unity which undergoes no division, but which is shared in by many. Soul affects it participants but the participants have no reciprocal effect upon Soul. This theme is further developed in terms of Soul's distribution of its powers. Employing an image that is prominent in his account of Soul's distention in time (*Ennead* III.7(45).ll.15-23), Plotinus now likens Soul to a seed that contains a great potential for growth but remains a self-gathered unity.[7] The powers of Soul are allocated to various parts of the body so that there are separate faculties of sensation, growth, and reason.

At the start of the final chapter of *Ennead* IV.9(8), Plotinus restates the central question of the treatise: therefore, how is there one substance in many souls (πῶς οὖν οὐσία μία ἐν πολλαῖς)? He considers two alternatives: either one nature is present in its entirety in all things or a multiplicity of natures is derived from one source which remains unaffected. Plotinus accepts the latter alternative as the most plausible explanation: like a science whose various branches are subsumed under one overarching discipline, Soul maintains its identity in spite of its thoroughgoing omnipresence, constituting a unity-in-plurality. [8]

The foregoing arguments are further developed in the later *Ennead* IV.3(27). In its opening chapter, Plotinus argues against those who maintain that our souls also came from the Soul of the All (νῦν δὲ πάλιν επανίωμεν ἐπὶ τοὺς λέγοντας ἐκ τῆς τοῦ παντὸς ψυχῆς καὶ τὰς ἡμετέρας εἶναι).[9] Denying that souls are segments of a higher entity, he affirms that it is more fitting to say that they are the same and one and that each soul is all (ἀλλὰ μᾶλλον ἂν τὴν αὐτὴν καὶ μίαν ἑκάστην πᾶσαν δικαιότερον ἂν εἴποιεν).[10]

When Plotinus denies that souls are "parts" of a higher Soul, he uses the term "part" (μερισμός) in a qualified sense. Partition implies a diminishing of a greater whole: the part is less than the whole. Since souls are all of the same nature, Soul as a totality cannot be partitioned off like a spatial magnitude or physical body. Soul is not fragmented or dispersed once embodied; the same Soul is omnipresent throughout Nature. The World Soul and individual souls are thus related to Soul as an entirety: they maintain their unity, like a light which spreads far and wide, emanating from one common source.

The participation relationship between Soul and its lower phases is analogous to that between the One and the universe of being. Like the One, Soul is never divided. If Soul appears to undergo division, it is only because of its omnipresence; Soul is present as an entirety in every participant. Neither Soul nor its lower phases is localized in the material cosmos or in individuals. Indeed, Soul cannot be considered in such spatial terms, that is, it is not "contained" in the universe or in individuals as wine is contained in a vessel. Such an analogue is flawed, because it suggests that the participant receives only a portion of Soul, just as the vessel can receive only a limited amount of liquid. In actuality, it is Soul which provides the "container," and the universe which constitutes the "contained.' Soul engulfs the universe as a whole, or to use Plotinus's own image, it is like a vast sea embracing and permeating a net.[11] But just as the net can stretch only to a certain extent, the universe has a limited capacity to participate in Soul's totality.

The Problem of Soul: A Working Hypothesis

However, although Plotinus clearly upholds the oneness of Soul, his psychological treatises pose something of a problem for the reader. This problem stems from Plotinus's frequent inconsistencies in defining the relationship between the third hypostasis itself, the World Soul, and individual souls. In *Ennead* IV.4(28).29.44-49, Plotinus recognizes the difficulties involved in dealing with the various aspects of Soul. As he sees it, the issue is whether the lower phases proceed from a higher level of Soul or whether every phase is independent of the others. In other words, the question addresses whether all souls are one and if so, how the many are related to this overriding unity.[12]

But the *Enneads* fail to provide any straightforward answer to such questions. Instead, Plotinus's psychological deliberations are permeated with conjecture and hypothesis; his conclusions seem tentative rather than dogmatic.[13] Accordingly, no interpretation of this aspect of Plotinian thought can hope to be more than speculative in tone. This point is made by Henry Blumenthal, who develops an effective methodology for dealing with Plotinus's psychological theory.[14] Rather than ignoring or attempting to explain away the inconsistencies, Blumenthal examines them more closely and considers their scope and extent. Since he offers the most detailed and well-reasoned account of this problem, I am adopting Blumenthal's interpretation as a kind of "working hypothesis" for the purposes of this study.

At the outset, Blumenthal presents what he perceives as the central issue regarding the problem of Soul in the *Enneads*:

Most discussions of the relations between different kinds of soul on the one hand, and between different souls of one kind or the other, are concerned with what they do rather than what they are. This in itself is significant, because most of what Ploltinus says is relevant only to the first of these questions. Though he devotes a certain amount of space to the proposition that all souls are one, he is more concerned with establishing their similarity than defining their differences. When the differences are important, they are either assumed or attributed to what are perhaps improperly described as extraneous influences. [15]

The overriding concern, therefore, is the *activity* of each so-called type or "kind" of Soul, rather than the fundamental differences between them. This appears to be a skillful way of upholding Plotinus's affirmation of Soul's unicity. We have seen that in a strict sense, only Soul exists for Plotinus. But Soul's unicity manifests itself in different ways on different ontological and psychological levels. The differences between such "phases" of Soul emerges when Plotinus considers the divergent activities of Soul as one. The "differences" do not point to any divergent natures possessed by the World Soul or individual souls. In the final analysis, all souls are of the same nature; they are properly distinguished on the basis of their focus and the intensity of their commitment to lower levels of reality.

Blumenthal further offers convincing textual evidence that the phrase "ἡ τοῦ παντὸς ψυχή" (Soul of the All) and its equivalent "ἡ τοῦ ὅλου ψυχή" (Soul of the Whole) refer to the lower aspect of the hypostasis Soul. The clarification of this point is rather important, since standard translations can be quite misleading in regard to their renderings of these phrases and this terminology.[16] In *Ennead* IV.9, Plotinus considers two possibilities: (1) souls are one because they come from "ἡ τοῦ παντὸς ψυχή" or (2) the "τοῦ παντος ψυχη" as well as individual souls come from one Soul and are one. Blumenthal queries as to whether "ἡ τοῦ παντὸς Ψυχή" is equivalent to "Ψυχή," the undifferentiated hypostasis of Soul itself.[17] The problem lies in determining if there exists a direct line of descent from (1) the hypostasis (Ψυχή) to (2) Soul of the All (ψυχή τοῦ παντός) to (3) individual souls, or whether individual souls and the Soul of the All both proceed from the hypostasis itself.

In various passages, Plotinus asserts that many souls are derived from one (*Enneads* IV.9.4, 15-18; IV.8.3, 11-12; III.9.3, 4-

5). These passages, however, are inexplicit as to what this "one" is and fail to specify whether the World Soul is included among the many "souls." The difficulties only amplify when one considers those passages in which the World Soul is called the "sister" of individual souls (*Enneads* IV.6, 13; II.9.18, 16). This designation seems to suggest a coequal status between World Soul and individual souls.

Perhaps a partial resolution to this problem is found in *Enneads* IV.4(28).32.4-13 and IV.3(27).4, 14-16, where Plotinus refers to a higher level of Soul than that which is characterized as Soul of the All (ψυχὴ τοῦ παντός). These passages establish the derivative nature of both the Soul of the All and the Soul of the Whole (ἡ τοῦ ὅλου ψυχή), both of which refer to the same entity. The hypostasis Soul (Ψυχή) must be interpreted as a unity whose various activities and foci demand even further distinctions (i.e., distinctions between the World Soul and individual souls). Such distinctions, in and of themselves, do not contradict Plotinus's affirmation that all souls are one. Like individual souls, the World Soul proceeds from a higher totality.[18]

The traditional approach to Soul's phases can be expressed by means of a vertical model, wherein the World Soul and individual souls are subordinated to the hypostasis:

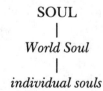

SOUL
|
World Soul
|
individual souls

While it does establish the derivative character of the World Soul and individual souls, such a model is inadequate because of its static quality. It implies that Soul's lower manifestations are ontologically "less" than the hypostasis from which they are derived. But if the World Soul and individual souls are any "less" than the hypothesis, it is not because of a difference in their natures. Rather, their subordinate status is based upon the fact that they exhibit a greater degree of commitment to (and involvement in) the material cosmos. In contrast, the model which I am adopting suggests a triangular relationship, whereby World Soul and individual souls proceed from the hypothesis *together*. In this model, the hypostasis stands at the apex and its lower manifestations are distributed along the base:

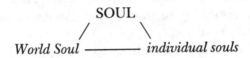

This model finds textual support in Plotinus's own assertion (*Ennead* IV.9.4.1-6) that all souls proceed from one Soul. Elsewhere (*Enneads* V.1(10).2.44; IV.3(27).6.1), Plotinus describes the World Soul as sharing the *same nature* (ὁμειδής) with individual souls. Still, Plotinus provides no definitive criteria for distinguishing between the various levels, phases, or "types" of Soul just discussed. But in view of the strong textual support for the contention that Plotinus upheld the unicity of Soul, it would appear that any real distinctions between Soul, World Soul, and individual souls are unwarranted.

Relevance Of Hypothesis For Soul's *Tolma*

This hypothesis assumes a special relevance when applied to the issue regarding the role of *tolma* in the emergence of the third hypostasis (and its lower phases). A salient teaching in Plotinus's psychological deliberations is that Soul's power diminishes increasingly as it becomes more particularized and more preoccupied with the material order. In Plotinian terms, living things are not only souls, but diminutions of souls, experiencing a gradual weakening of life and power as they move farther from their divine origin.[19]

While the World Soul governs the material cosmos in a remote, detached manner, the individual soul is more directly involved with physical reality. Plotinus thus distinguishes between the operation of the hypostasis in its supervision of the totality and its commitment to an individual sphere of commitment.[20]   In some places, Plotinus describes this involvement with an individual body in negative terms as a debasement and deprecation.

But both the downward focus of the World Soul and the embodiment of individual souls can be viewed as expressions of a movement which permeates the Plotinian universe. This movement, as we have seen, originates in *Nous* and results in the emergence of reality other than the One. The *tolma* or will toward otherness which underlies and sustains *Nous* provides the basis of otherness and differentiation throughout Plotinus's metaphysical scheme. On the level of Soul, expressions of *tolma* operate in a manner analogous to what is found on the level of *Nous*. Again, *tolma* is responsible for an estrangement of a lower from a higher ontological principle. Soul enters into increasing levels of diversity and individuation; this movement culminates in a more direct involvement on the part of Soul with temporal process and material bodies. In contrast to *Nous's* timeless contemplation of the One, Soul engages in discursive reasoning, relying upon images for knowledge and passing from one object to another.

In view of Plotinus's clear affirmation of the unicity of Soul, it would appear that the presence of *tolma* can rightfully be attributed to the *hypostasis as a whole*. This, I think, is a crucial point which commentators seem to have overlooked. Instead, *tolma* on the level of Soul has been attributed only to individual souls, as if these represented independent psychological principles that have no relationship to either the World Soul or to the hypostasis Soul as an entirety. On the basis of some key Plotinian texts, however, I believe one is justified in linking Plotinus's account of Soul's temporalization with his general account of the descent of individual souls into material bodies. On the basis of these preliminary considerations, let us now assess the role of Soul's *tolma* in greater depth.

Notes

1. *Ennead* IV.8(6).7.1-14. cf. *Enneads* II.3(52).17.15-25; IV.6(41).3.1-16.

2. *Ennead* V.1(10).3.10-25.   cf. *Enneads* V.1(10).10.1-10;   V.4(49).9.23-26;
   V.6(24).4.14-20; V.8(31).13.11-15; V.1(10).7.36-42; V.2(11).1.1-21.

3. *Ennead* IV.9(8).1.1-13.

4. *Ennead* V.5(32).9.29-33.

5. *Enneads* V.8(31).12.12-26; III.8(30).5.10-22.

6. *Ennead* IV.9(8).1.1-9.

7. *Ennead* IV.9(8).5.1-11.

8. *Ennead* IV.9(8).5.12-28.

9. *Ennead* IV.3(27).1.16-18.

10. *Enneads* IV.3(27).2.3-5; IV.3(27).5.8-18; VI.4(22).14.1-7.

11. *Ennead* IV.3(27).9.34-44.

12. *Ennead* IV.4(28).29.44-55.

13. The speculative character of the deliberations is often revealed in state-
    ments expressing doubt or invoking divine assistance.   cf. *Enneads*
    IV.9(9).5.26-28;   IV.9(9).4.6-8;   III.7(45).11.9-11   (the   passage   which
    discusses the World Soul's generation of temporal process and relies
    upon mythical imagery in expressing its main themes).

14. Henry Blumenthal, "Soul, World-Soul, and Individual Soul in Plotinus,"
    Le Néoplatonisme (Royaument, 1969), pp. 55-66. (Hereafter referred to as
    "Soul.") Blumenthal further develops these insights in the later paper
    "Nous and Soul in Plotinus," in *Plotino e il Neoplatonismo*, 1974, pp. 203-
    219.
    cf. Blumenthal, "Soul," p. 56: "I should like to say . . . that I am not going
    to produce a solution out of the hat. For whatever reasons Plotinus does
    not provide us with necessary material. The purpose of this paper is
    merely to examine what Plotinus does say, to look more closely at the
    inconsistencies . . . and . . . consider their extent." (Blumenthal here cites

Zeller's *Die Philosophie der Griechen* III, ii (Leipzig, 1881), p. 542, n. 4, which addressed this very issue at an earlier date.)

15. Blumenthal, "Soul," p. 56.

16. Stephen MacKenna's translation provides a case in point, referring to these phrases as "All Soul," an appellation which might also designate the hypostasis Soul, the totality of souls. Armstrong, on the other hand, tends to avoid making distinctions, using the generic term "Soul" to designate the various phases. I favor Armstrong's approach in my own discussion of the varieties of Soul and their operation.

17. Blumenthal, "Soul," p. 56: "Does Plotinus distinguish two kinds of soul, the individual soul and the ψυχή τοῦ παντός and ψυχή without qualification?"

18. cf. Enneads IV.3(27).6.12 ("πᾶσα ψυχή"); III.2(47).4. 10-11 ("ὅλη ψυχή"). Blumenthal also cites passages (in "Soul," p. 58) which suggest that the World Soul follows immediately after *Nous* (*Ennead* II.3.7.18). In those passages, the World Soul has direct access to *Nous*. This does not rule out the existence of the hypostasis Soul. It merely describes the demiurgic functions of Soul and *Nous*. Such passages emphasize the relation between *Nous* and the lower levels of Soul which Plotinus designates as "φύσις." In this connection, he provides this thought-provoking insight: ". . . there is no need to conclude from the fact that Plotinus does distinguish the hypostasis Soul and the World Soul that we are to envisage a series of five hypostases, the One, Nous, World Soul, and its lower part . . ."

19. *Ennead* III.3(48).3.24-29.

20. cf. *Ennead* IV.8(6).4.1-10.

Chapter IV

The *Tolma* of Soul

As we have seen, the *tolma* of *Nous* is responsible for the emergence of multiplicity. *Nous* contains within itself the world of Forms, a highly concentrated unity-in-plurality admitting of neither division nor spatial distinction of any kind. This aggregate engages in an eternal contemplation of the One, enjoying an immediate intuition of truth. Soul's *tolma* prompts a severance from this noetic level. The immediate result of Soul's *tolma* is the initiation of time, an act whereby an aspect or principle of Soul becomes temporalized, thereby subjecting itself to the demands of change and process.

Plotinus's attribution of *tolma* (or, an "unquiet nature") to Soul is found in two key places: *Enneads* III.7(45).11(15-23) and V.1(10).1(1-10). In the former passage, *tolma*-language is not explicitly used, but Plotinus speaks of the motive for descent in terms of a restless, disquieting principle that can be easily interpreted in tolmatic terms. Accordingly, *Ennead* III.7(45).11 should rightfully be considered in conjunction with the earlier *Ennead* V.1(10).1, where Plotinus attributes the substantive *tolma* to the dynamics of souls' descent toward temporal process and ultimately, their material embodiment.[1] In both passages, the overall context and motive for descent are the same: principles of the hypostasis Soul (i.e., World Soul and individual souls) seek self-determination through a willful act. In this sense, the descent of the World Soul and that of individual souls can be considered as aspects of the same downward movement from the contemplative life of *Nous* to different levels of temporal involvement.[2]

The repurcussions of Soul's *tolma* are far-reaching: it establishes an antithetical relationship between eternity and time, and by implication, between the life of contemplation and that of action. The lower phases of Soul are separated from the life of *Nous*, the godlike image of the One. This severance assumes, in Plotinus's language, the proportions of a defection or revolt. In one passage, he asserts that Soul would remain with the divine if it were not for an intentional apostasy, that is, "unless it desires to stand apart" (τῇ δὲ ὑπάρχει ἐν τούτοις εἶναι συναφθείσῃ, εἰ μὴ ἀποστατεῖν ἐθέλοι).[3] Elsewhere, he characterizes Soul's tendency toward differentiation in similar terms: the division itself is referred to as an apostasy (καὶ γὰρ ὁ μερισμὸς αὐτῆς τὸ ἀποστῆναι).[4] This characterization calls to mind the language of Ennead VI.9(9).5.29, where Plotinus describes *Nous* as "standing apart" from the One (ἀποστῆναι δέ πως ἑνὸς τολμήσας). In both instances, Plotinus seems to take a dim view of the drive toward otherness. The movement itself he roots in an act of *tolma*. *Nous* and Soul are both guilty of estranging themselves from higher principles of unity. In the theological language of the Neopythagoreans and the Gnostics, such *tolma* might be viewed as constituting an audacious usurpation of a divine prerogative. In the case of Soul, however, the defection is more pronounced, because *tolma* prompts an abandonment of the self-contained life of eternity and contemplation in favor of a more fragmented mode of being.

The Genesis of Soul

Plotinus treats the first manifestation of *tolma* on the level of Soul (i.e., as World Soul) in *Ennead* III.7(45).11, in the treatise on *"Eternity and Time"*. The passage in question provides an explicit account of Soul's incursion into the temporal order. This constitutes the beginning of the World Soul's involvement with the material cosmos, and ultimately, its entry into human existence. In Plotinian terms, Soul provides the vital link between the noetic and material orders, exhibiting a dual focus: while it is related essentially to *Nous* and the intelligible world, it directs itself downward in governing and supervising Nature. [5]

Ennead III.7(45).11 is a passage highly flavored with mythical imagery.[6] Plotinus appears to realize that he is venturing into an uncertain area. The speculative nature of the deliberations is reflected in the methodology which he employs, personalizing time and suggesting that we ask time itself how it originated. The account which follows assumes the form of what time would say if prompted to comment upon its origin. The analysis proceeds in a manner similar to that which Plotinus applies to *Nous*. Just as *Nous* was depicted as somehow existing in the One prior to its generation (*Ennead* III.8(30).8.32-38) time is described as already existing in eternity. Such attempts at dramatization are indicative of the profound difficulties involved in conceptualizing and describing aspects of the spiritual world.[7] But Plotinus's methodology also suggests the ontological "distance" between time and eternity. He continually resorts to spatial and temporal metaphors in explaining the transition between the two orders.

In keeping with Plato's *Timaeus* account (37D-38B), Plotinus views time as the extension of the life of eternity, distinguishing between eternity (as the unified life of contemplation) and time (as the fragmented life of change, action, and discursive reasoning). In *Ennead* III.7(45).13.23-28, Plotinus directly refers to Plato (*Timaeus* 38B6-C2; 37D4-C7) in defining time as the paradigm and moving image of eternity. For motion and process are intimately related to the temporal order. In contrast, eternity is the life which exists fully and completely in authentic being. By its very nature, eternity is connected with the intelligible order, centered around the One and gravitating toward its stabilizing presence. Plotinus exalts eternity as something sacred, identifying it with *Nous*, which he likens to a god. [8]

Ennead III.7(45).11 begins with a restatement of the characterization of eternity presented in the early chapters of the treatise, that is, a serene life, complete, without boundaries or movement. Before time existed, it enjoyed such a stable condition, knowing neither priority nor succession. But a restless nature was present, Plotinus asserts, which sought self-determination and autonomy (Φύσεως δὲ πολυπράγμονος καὶ ἄρχειν αυτῆς βουλομένης καὶ εἶναι αὐτῆς). Soul, we are informed, desired more than its present state, that is, more than it found in eternity. This restless nature initiated a movement concomitant with the origin of time.

In contrast to the stable and motionless life of eternity, time is characterized by diversity and change. In Plotinian terms,

Soul opts for the novelty of succession and a continuous sequence of events and activities. In figurative terms, we embark on a long, drawn-out course or journey, constructing time as a copy or image of eternity (μῆκός τι τῆς πορείας ποιησάμενοι αἰῶνος εἰκόνα τὸν Χρόνον εἰργάσμεθα).[9]

Soul's gravitation toward the manifold displays a continuity with *Nous's* desire to possess all things (αὐτὸν πάντα ἔχειν θέλων). Both *Nous* and Soul attempt to over-extend their proper range of activities: *Nous* desires to be other than the One; Soul seeks the sequential patterning that characterizes time, action, and discursive reasoning. Two factors contribute to Soul's culpability. First, Soul "temporalizes" itself by making time in imitation of eternity (πρῶτον μὲν ἑαυτὴν ἐχρόνωσεν ἀντὶ τοῦ αἰῶνος τοῦτον ποιήσασα). Secondly, Soul makes being subservient to the demands of temporality. Figuratively, it "enslaves" being to time (ἔπειτα δὲ καὶ τῷ γενομένῳ ἔδωκε δουλεύειν χρόνῳ), placing it in a temporal context. Since the world moves in Soul, and Soul becomes temporalized, the world itself becomes temporalized. In effect, time and the material cosmos come into existence simultaneously.[10]

Plotinus's coining of the verb "ἐχρόνασεν" in this discussion is significant. By virtue of its use, he seems to imply that an aspect or power of Soul (i.e., World Soul as "δύναμις τῆς ψυχῆς") *becomes time*. In this respect, it would be erroneous to maintain that Soul "*entered into*" time or even that it "*descended into*" the material cosmos. Such assertions suggest that time exists independently of Soul. But this is clearly not the case in Plotinian terms. As he later states, one must not apprehend time as something existing outside of the life of Soul (Δεῖ δὲ οὐκ ἔξωθεν τῆς ψυχῆς λαμβάνειν τον Χρόνον). Time is not a co-principle or appendage of Soul, but something which emerges along with Soul and which exists in and with it ('αλλ ἐνορώμενον καὶ ἐνόντα καὶ συνόντα). Soul generates time as a result of its activity.[11]   This activity effects the transition between the eternal and the temporal modes of being.

At the conclusion of *Ennead* III.7(45).ll.43-45, Plotinus presents his most complete definition of time, that is, the life of Soul in a transitional movement (Ψυχῆς ἐν κινήσει μεταβατικῇ) from one way of life to another (ἐξ ἄλλου εἰς ἄλλον βίον ζωὴν

εἶναι). Thus, time is a life different from that of eternity—
mobile, impermanent, and fragmented. In contrast to the life of
Nous, the life of Soul engages in a sequential ordering of
thought and action. It is characterized by discursive reasoning
(ἡ διάνοια) and a continuous succession of events. While
eternal life is a unified, self-contained whole, time represents
a distention or diffusion of life (διάστασις ζωῆς). As such, it
constitutes a mere imitation of a more authentic mode of
being.[12]

At the base of Soul's movement lies an act of *tolma*, the audacious drive toward otherness and separate existence. In *Ennead*
III.7(45).11, this will assumes the form of a restless inquietude
which is the expression of Soul's dissatisfaction with its mode of
existence. As Soul "wearies" of its participation in the noetic
world, it seeks to create actively on its own, shifting its focus to
the supervision of the material cosmos as a whole. In so doing,
it assumes the role of World Soul, the downward facing, active
power of the third hypostasis in Plotinus's metaphysical scheme.

The Significance of "*Polupragmon*" (Πολυπράγμων)

In regard to Plotinus's discussion of Soul's temporalization,
closer attention must be paid to the phrase "Φύσεως δὲ
πολυπράγμονον," which Armstrong translates as a "restlessly
active nature." The term *polupragmonon* (πολυπράγμονοων) is
rather rich in meaning, assuming a number of connotations that
are relevant to an appreciation of its use in *Ennead* III.7(45).11.
In its most literal sense, *polupragmon*, an adjectival construction
derived from the verb *polupragmoneo* (πολυπραγμονέω), designates "doing many things" or more precisely, "being busy after
many things at once." In concrete terms, it refers to an
officious, meddlesome, or fastidious character, or to an over-
excessive concern with many details at the same time.[13] This
meaning is reflected in the earliest uses of the term, where it
served as an epithet attributable to annoying busybodies or to
troublesome gadflies.[14] But *polupragmon* also assumed an epistemological import, designating a curiosity for knowledge of all
kinds. In some places, it means "curious" in the rather positive
sense of an interest in factual information of an historical,

geographical, or scientific nature.[15] While such a wide-ranging curiosity is certainly not blameworthy, it assumed a wholly negative connotation in later writings, where it implied a prying or aimless inquisitiveness or a frivolous interest in all things at once, and hence, a mastery of none. [16]

In Plato, the verb *polupragmoneo* (πολυπραγμονέω) assumed a pronounced political connotation. *The Republic* employs the term in a discussion of Justice (δικαιοσύνη) one of the four classical Greek virtues, along with Temperance (σωφροσύνη), Courage (ανδρεία), and Wisdom (σοφια). As Plato asserts, ". . . to do one's own business and not to be a busybody is Justice . . ."[17] In this sense, true Justice involves a harmonization of the various levels of the State, whereby the parts work together for the good of the whole. But if Justice is defined as the "principle of doing one's own business," injustice is its direct antithesis, and proceeds from the encroachment of one group or class upon the interests or tasks proper to another. The very act of "being a busybody" creates an unjust situation, that is, the "interference with another business" which constitutes the "greatest injury to the State . . ."[18] Thus, the "polupragmatic" tendency (if I might coin the term) underlies a condition of discord, strife, and imbalance that prompts an overstepping of bounds or a subversion of one's proper station.

In Plotinus, *polupragmon* is transposed to a higher metaphysical plane. In contrast to Plato, the highest Plotinian virtues are not the civic ones, but those which assist in the soul's purification from bodily influences.[19] In effect, Plotinus transformed Plato's civic virtues into contemplative ones (cf. *Ennead* I.4). In Plotinian terms, true virtue is found in that which is conducive to contemplation and the grasp of intuitive knowledge. Conversely, evil proceeds from that which hinders the contemplative life. The "polupragmatic" tendency assumes such a hindering role.

As we have just observed, Plotinus's most prominent reference to this "polupragmatic" tendency on the part of Soul is found in *Ennead* III.7(45).11.15-20. But the "restlessly active nature" to which Plotinus refers in that passage might be viewed in two ways. First, Soul's restlessness can be interpreted as purely passive, suggesting a boredom or *ennui* which disaffects

Soul from Nous and the life of contemplation. Secondly, Soul's restlessness can assume a more dynamic role, prompting it to act in response to a prior sense of alienation. *Ennead* III.7(45).11.15-17 implies that Soul's commitment to the contemplative life of eternity weakens. In its place, Soul opts for self-determination: as Plotinus says, it "desired to govern itself and be independent" (καὶ ἄρχειν αὐτῆς βουλομένης καὶ εἶναι αὐτῆς). But this desire presupposes a dissatisfaction on Soul's part with what it already possesses. It thereby chooses to seek more than it presently has (τὸ πλέον τοῦ παρόντος ζητεῖν ἑλομένης).

Some fifteen treatises earlier (in terms of Porphyry's chronology), Plotinus used a similar image to describe Nous's severance from the One. *Ennead* III.8(30).8 discusses Nous's descent in terms of the same movement, insofar as it responds to a desire for more than it possesses. In *Ennead* III.8(30).8.34, Plotinus relied upon the quantitative metaphor of "weight": *Nous*, it relates, grew "heavy" as if drowsy, bored or intoxicated and "unravelled itself" (ἐξείλιξεν αὐτὸν), becoming variegated and multiple in the process.[20] *Ennead* III.7(45).11.24 employs a variation of this theme in discussing Soul's gravitation toward the temporal manifold: "uncoiling itself" (ἐξειλίττων αὐτόν) like a seed, Soul attempts to actualize its innate potentialities, spreading itself outward in imitation of eternity. Just as the seed expands its powers, Soul unrolls, divides, and disperses in temporal process, containing within itself the virtuality of all subsequent things.[21]

But this expansion results in a squandering of Soul's faculties, constituting a distention that is characterized at *Ennead* III.7(45).11.26-27 as a "going forth to a weaker greatness" (εἰς μῆκος ἀσθενέστερον πρόεισιν). Soul thus subjects itself to the demands of the spatio-temporal order and its accompanying laws: discursive reasoning replaces noetic contemplation and the temporal succession of events (in terms of "before" and "after") supplants the full possession of life found in eternity.

In keeping with a key connotation of *polupragmon*, Plotinus associates an element of curiosity with Soul's restlessness in this context. Soul's downward orientation draws it away from the stability of eternal contemplation, directing it toward the novelty and change inherent in the temporal order. Soul reacts against the sameness of eternity, "always moving on to...what is not the same." In this regard, Soul's "unquiet power" or "restless nature" displays a kinship with *tolma*, which likewise connotes a venturesomeness or indiscreet curiosity to know what is not one's proper concern or what is improper for the human intellect to know. [22]

While *Ennead* III.7(45).11 makes no explicit reference to *tolma*, its language (like that of *Ennead* III.8(30).8) strongly suggests an assertiveness that calls to mind a tolmatic act of will. In this respect, we see a continuity between the "unquiet power" of Soul discussed in *Ennead* III.7(45).11.20-23 and the *tolma* which Plotinus posits as the primary motive for the descent of individual souls into material bodies. In effect, *tolma* prompts the severance of the World Soul and individual souls from the life of *Nous*. Once detached from the intellectual cosmos, these lower phases of Soul assume different roles. Their downward orientation entails (1) the supervision of the universe as a whole; and (2) the supervision of individual entities. [23] The second type of supervision involves the descent of souls into material bodies. This movement will now be investigated.

The *Tolma* of Individual Souls

The World Soul, as we have seen, exercises an all-encompassing concern for the material cosmos, governing from a "distance" (to use a spatial metaphor not entirely applicable to the spiritual order) and therefore, not directly involved with that which it supervises. As a means of describing the World Soul's relationship with lower reality, Plotinus uses the analogy of the architect who designs and oversees a beautiful, elaborate dwelling place from afar, not actually living in the structure. [24] At most then, it maintains a kind of "casual acquaintance" with Nature: its role lies in communicating form and intelligibility to the lowest levels of the hierarchy of being.

In contrast, individual souls have a more pronounced commitment to the material cosmos. Their *tolma* carries them into a direct association with corporeal natures, whereby they engage, in Plotinus's language, in a personal, "hands on" supervision (αὐτουργῷ τινι ποιήσει ουναφῇ). The World Soul's thoroughgoing interest in the administration of the totality is narrowed down to a particular sphere of concern. By attaching themselves to material beings, individual souls are subject to a plethora of bodily passions, emotions, and other desires. In keeping with a common Greek religious belief, Plotinus depicts souls as tending to the bodily counterpart with which they are most compatible. Ontologically, they remain independent of matter, always retaining their tie with the intelligible world. But the quality of the soul's supervision and its effectiveness as a rational principle is dependent upon the matter with which it associates itself. The body becomes the medium whereby souls extend themselves deeper and deeper into the grip of bodily influences.[25]

In *Ennead* V.1(10).1.1-10, we find Plotinus's central statement regarding the descent of individual souls into matter, as well as the *locus classicus* of *tolma*-language in the *Enneads*. Souls' *tolma* is another, but more intense expression of the will toward otherness which underlies the entire process of emanation. The will toward otherness precipitates a general movement from unity to multiplicity, from universality to particularity. At the highest level of Plotinus's metaphysical scheme is the One: remote, simple, and perfect in every respect. At the other extreme lies matter, almost completely devoid of the efficacy of being. Individual souls tend to this outermost extreme. *Ennead* V.1(10).1.1-10 (and the closely related *Ennead* IV.8) come to terms with this movement.[26]

The Role of *Tolma* in *Ennead* V.1(10).1

Plotinus begins *Ennead* V.1(10).1 with a question, asking what it was that prompted souls to forget the divine father and, although members of the divine world, to be completely ignorant of their true natures and their origin. The answer to this initial question immediately follows:

... the origin of evil for them is *tolma* (Ἀρχὴ μὲν οὖν αὐταῖς τοῦ κακοῦ ἡ τόλμα), in the tendency toward temporal generation and otherness (καὶ ἡ γένεσις καὶ ἡ πρώτη ἑτερότης) and in the desire to be on their own (καὶ τὸ βουληθῆναι δὲ ἑαυτων εἶναι). Taking delight in this free-

dom of self-determination, they made great use of their movement: they
ran along the wrong course and stood apart from the father at a great
distance, forgetting that they had come from the divine place. [27]

In addition to *tolma, Ennead* V.1(10).1 thus suggests several
other motives for the souls' descent. All of these, however, are
ultimately rooted in *tolma,* with its connotations of audacity and
apostasy. The descent itself is described in volitional terms. In
this respect, one finds a suggestion of sin or moral error. But
tolma also thrusts the lower phases of the hypostasis Soul into
temporal process, that is, souls are motivated by a desire for
generation and otherness. This desire, it will be remembered, is
also prominent in the distention of World Soul (as depicted in
Ennead III.7(45).11.15-23). Thus, Plotinus's discussion of the
descent of individual souls exhibits a close alliance and kinship
with both *Ennead* III.7(45).11.15-23 and with his treatment of
Nous's severance from the One in *Enneads* VI.9(9).5.24-29,
III.8(30).8.31-38, and V.8(31).13.1-11. In this sense, the seces-
sion of *Nous* initiates a general movement toward otherness
throughout the universe of being. The *tolma* of Soul on all of its
levels is associated with this initial drive toward otherness.

Soul's *tolma* also manifests itself as a desire for self-determination: souls sin through an act of will directed toward self-ownership. They wish to be on their own and to function as creative
principles in their own right, descending, as Plotinus says, with a
"great zeal" (προθυμία δὲ πλείονι) into the material order. Like
the World Soul, individual souls seek to actualize untapped
potentialities, desiring more than they already possess. Unlike
the World Soul, however, they shift their focus from the supervision of the totality to become partial and self-centered
(μεταβάλλουσαι δὲ ἐκ τοῦ ὅλου εἰς τὸ μέρος τε ἐῖναι καὶ
ἑαυτῶν).[28]   As a result, their· intellective powers are fragmented and dispersed. As in the case of the World Soul, individual souls distend themselves in multifarious activities and
concerns. Their isolation, however, is more extreme, since they
must desert the totality to pursue their own independent
courses.

Once again, we find a suggestion of alienation even prior to
actual descent. In *Ennead* IV.8(6).4.10-21. Plotinus informs us
that souls withdraw in a great distress or turmoil to occupy

some other station, taking great delight in their freedom of movement. But how can souls weary of their participation in the perfectly stable, self-contained life of *Nous*? The determinant is will, which prompts souls to "stand apart" at a great distance. Succumbing to an irrational element within their own nature, they gravitate toward inferior levels of reality, experiencing a kind of "guilt by association," and assuming the inferior quality of the objects of their devotion.

An Additional Motive

Another key motive for the descent of individual souls is a narcissistic self-love. This theme is closely connected with motifs which emerge in *Ennead* V.1(10).1.1-10: souls desire self-determination and tend toward the realm of change, motion, and differentiation in search of a fuller realization of latent potentialities. In *Ennead* IV.4(28).3, Plotinus considers the role of a narcissistic element in the descent of the soul which departs from the intelligible world. Unable to endure that prior unity, it loves itself, desiring to be other and tending outward.[29] Elsewhere, Plotinus develops this theme in a mythical context.

Ennead IV.3(27).12 refers to the allegorical account of the boy who, seeing his image in a pool of water and staring into that "mirror of Dionysius," toppled in and drowned. In a similar manner, souls "see" their images in bodies and enter the corporeal realm in an impulsive surge.[30] In the very act of "seeing their images," souls become enamoured with their own creative potential. The images or "idols" (εἴδωλα) to which Plotinus refers are the bodies which souls are destined to govern. In this discussion, souls gravitate toward the non-being of matter as if enchanted; bodies provide fresh prospects for creativity on an individual basis. But like the reflection in Dionysius's "mirror," these material prospects are deceptive. For in its direct involvement with corporeal nature, the soul is subjected to all of the cares, anxieties, and vicissitudes of human existence.

Lower Manifestations of *Tolma*

Human bodies are not the only terminus of souls driven by *tolma*. The will toward otherness also carries them into more inferior corporeal entities (i.e., animals and plants) and even manifests itself in brute, formless matter. This is borne out in several passages. In *Ennead* V.2(11).2 (immediately following *Ennead* V.1(10).1 in chronological order), Plotinus employs the adjectival form of the substantive *tolma* in describing the entry of souls into vegetal and animal life.

> When, therefore, the soul becomes a plant what is in the plant is another part of it of sorts, the most audacious (τὸ τολμηρότατον) and foolish part of it and that which has advanced to this extent; when it advances in irrational life, the power to perceive through the senses dominated and led it.[31]

Ennead I.8(51).9.18-19 further employs *tolma*-language in designating the act whereby the human intellect directs itself toward matter. Because matter is formless, it cannot provide the intellect with any intelligible content. By gazing upon formless matter, intellect likewise becomes formless. As in other passages, Plotinus adopts the basic tenet of Aristotelian psychology that the knower is identical with that which is known: if the object of knowledge is formless matter, then the recipient subject must be formless as well. Plotinus asserts that the intellect which gravitates toward matter is another intellect, which is not intellect at all, since it dares or ventures to see what is not its own (Διὸ καὶ νοῦς ἄλλος αὐτος, οὐ νοῦς, τολμήσας ἰδεῖν τὰ μη αὐτοῦ).

Here, the verb-form "τολμήσας" expresses a careless venturesomeness or restless curiosity (similar, in fact, to the connotation of *polupragmonon* at *Ennead* III.7(45).11.15) which propels intellect into an alien environment. Paradoxically, Plotinus likens this movement to the "vision" of darkness. While one cannot, properly speaking, see darkness, one can nonetheless experience it as a privation of light. So also, when the intellect directs itself toward the formlessness of matter, it abandons the "light" of being, embracing (in the context of Plotinus's analogy), the "darkness" or privation of matter, the direct antithesis of the One and its abundant goodness.[32]

In Plotinus's metaphysical scheme, matter is at the lowest level of the One's outflow. The material world represents the terminus in the chain of being which originates in the self-diffusiveness of the One, punctuated by a "will to otherness" or *tolma.* On the material level, we move into the very hinterlands of being, an ontological wasteland almost totally deprived of the One's power and life. Because of its ontological "distance" from the One, Plotinus characterizes matter as evil—"absolutely deficient" and nearly lacking in being.

For Plotinus, that which is absolutely deficient (i.e., matter) cannot have any real share in the good. While it must possess some kind of existence, its existence is one of privation, the opposite of rational form.[33]   But as in other key areas of his thought, Plotinus displays marked inconsistencies and an apparent incoherence here. In view of this, there are grounds for assuming a development of Plotinus's thought over an extended period of time on this topic. [34]

Still, Plotinus's treatment of matter prompts some questions from both a metaphysical and a moral standpoint. The optimistic attitude toward the material world presented in Plato's *Timaeus* is carried over into the *Enneads.* However, one also finds a devaluation of the material world in Plotinus and a markedly negative attitude toward matter itself. But the same inconsistency seems evident in Plato, whose optimism in the *Timaeus* was offset by the more pessimistic sentiments of the *Phaedrus* (246-247), where the soul's presence to the body was attributed to a kind of pre-natal fall. In addition, the *Theaetetus* (176A) localizes evil in "mortal nature and this earthly sphere."

This Platonic characterization of the material world as the abode of evil is also present in Plotinus, but with an important qualification. In Plotinian terms, matter is designated as evil because it is nearly devoid of the One's power. And, as Plotinus states, "that which has nothing because it is in want or rather is want, must necessarily be evil."[35] But in spite of its ontological deficiency, matter always maintains a vital contact with the spiritual order through the agency of the soul.

Matter itself exhibits a tolmatic surge. Plotinus addresses this point in *Ennead* III.6(26).14, where he identifies matter with "Poverty," a personalization of ontological privation.[36] Figuratively, matter represents the "poverty" of form and being; because of its ontological deficiency, it attempts to "seize" what it lacks through an act of *tolma.* In this context, *tolma* manifests itself as a presumptious desire to attain what cannot be attained,

namely, form and intelligibility. While matter provides a referent for being, it does not possess being.

The presence of *tolma* here is rather intriguing: since matter
represents the terminus of the Plotinian chain of being, *tolma*
on this level can only be directed "upward." For we find nothing
lower than matter or more inferior in Plotinus's universe.
Unlike the *tolma* of *Nous* and Soul, a will toward otherness which
is directed "downward" and away from the One, the *tolma* of
matter can only prompt it toward higher levels of reality and
increasing levels of unification. In fact, it must: because matter
constitutes the absolute end-point, any will that it exhibits gives
rise to a complementary movement toward reunification with
the One. This is the beginning of the ascent of being toward the
One, the *epistrophé* which counterbalances the *próodos* or outward procession and brings the Plotinian metaphysics to completion. (For a more detailed statement on this ascending
movement, the basis of Plotinian mysticism, see *Appendix A*,
"The Ascent to the One in Plotinus.")

The Concupiscential Element

As we have observed, matter for Plotinus constitutes the basis of
evil for the soul, the very antithesis of Goodness, Truth, and
Beauty. In its pure, unfallen state, the soul possessed a clear
vision of authentic reality. Once immersed in matter, however,
this vision is obscured and the soul's faculties are severely
impaired.[37] "This is the fall of the soul," Plotinus asserts, ". . .
to come to matter and to become feeble because all the powers
do not enter into operation . . ."[38] In this context, matter is
depicted as a kind of "lure" which draws the soul downward to
inferior reality by arousing its desire for sense images.

By associating with matter, the soul succumbs to the negative
influence of various vices. The most prominent of these is the
epithumia or lust which accompanies material involvements.
Such lust prompts an inner turbulence, tearing the soul in many
directions.[39] Plotinus's descriptions of the ill-effects of lust
occasionally assume a political tone which calls to mind Plato's
deliberations upon true Justice, the harmonization of the parts
of the State for the good of the whole. Conversely, injustice is a

condition of strife and discord, that "interference with one another's business."[40] For Plato, political injustice is analogous to moral disorder on an individual scale, an imbalance or upheaval which proceeds from reason's domination by the irrational appetites. Plotinus echoes these sentiments, likening the worst of men to a bad political constitution, an "inner rabble" of pleasures, desires, and fears.[41]

In these discussions, Plotinus interprets lust or concupiscence as the consequence rather than the direct cause of the soul's fall: without a body requiring sustenance, comfort, and pleasure, the soul would remain free of corporeal influences. As he affirms, ". . . for it is corporeal and such kind of body, it is hindered by every manner of change and possesses every kind of desire."[42]

But Plotinus also discusses another form of concupiscence, namely, the *prothumia* or "eager desire" which prompts the soul to gravitate toward matter. The passages in which this term appears stress both a voluntaristic and a deterministic character of the soul's descent: the soul descends because it desires to do so, but that desire is in accord with the dictates of cosmic necessity. As *Ennead* IV.8(6).5.3-8 states, ". . . necessity encompasses the voluntary . . . the voluntariness and the involuntariness of the descent." In effect, volition and necessity merge.

Plotinus relies upon some basic biological models to explicate this movement. The soul's *prothumia* for descent, he maintains, is as natural as physiological drives or growth processes. At the appropriate time, the soul descends in search of its proper place in the universe, and "with greater eager desire plunges in misery inside and does not remain whole with whole . . ."[43] The soul is carried along by a natural momentum to matter, a kind of "pain of childbirth to come there where that which is within them . . . tells them to come."[44]

But the movement whereby the soul descends is itself the culmination of a larger movement toward differentiation, otherness, and individuation on all levels of Plotinus's metaphysical scheme.[45] In this respect, *prothumia* exhibits some interesting parallels with *tolma*, the primary motive for the fall of individual souls as depicted in *Ennead* V.1(10).1.1-10. Both *tolma* and *prothumia* suggest an urge or impulse to engage in independent activity. *Tolma*, however, is described as a blame-worthy act while *prothumia* is viewed as a purely spontaneous response to the necessity of the soul's descent.

The Necessity of Soul's Descent

In a number of passages, Plotinus assumes a pessimistic posture toward Soul's descent. Statements explicitly using *tolma*-language (*Enneads* V.l(10).1.1-10; V.2(11).2.1-10) or language expressing the same sentiments (*Ennead* III.7(45).11.15-23) imply that descent is voluntary, carrying with it a degree of cul-pability. But a more optimistic view emerges in other places, such as those passages just considered, where Plotinus main-tains that Soul's descent is in perfect accord with the dictates of cosmic law. In this respect, Soul is depicted as "sent" to order the material cosmos, and on a lower level, human bodies, vege-tal forms, and animal life. From this standpoint, Soul's presence in the material cosmos is not necessarily an evil.

Ennead IV.8(6).5.3-8 represents an early attempt on Plotinus's part to link the volitional character of Soul's descent with a cosmic necessity. The innate propensity of the World Soul and individual souls for self-determination works in conjunction with a universal law. Thus, necessity merges with freedom of choice and paradoxically, descent is undertaken both willingly and unwillingly. On the one hand, descent is involuntary, con-stituting a direct response to the demands of law; on the other hand, descent is prompted by Soul's tendency for self-assertion. In this sense, Soul's incursion into the material cosmos is deemed blameworthy. Yet, even this seemingly volitional movement is consistent with law. In effect, it appears that Soul has no other choice but to descend so as to play its role in the inexorable process of emanation and so that it might actualize its potentialities through material embodiment. [46]

The later *Ennead* IV.3(27).13.7-22 completely eliminates the volitional element and binds Soul's descent exclusively to the demands of cosmic necessity. Souls are described as borne along by a natural momentum to the loci for which they are best suited. The descent is viewed as purely instinctive, occur-ring at the appropriate time, like the herald's calling (οἷον κήρυκος καλοῦντος). Plotinus, in fact, describes this desire for separation as completely spontaneous, comparing it to the natural inclination toward marriage or to the habitual performance of good acts. In this respect, souls are neither constrained by external influences nor given a choice between alternative courses of action. They do what they must at the right moment.

In keeping with his commitment to Hellenic rationalism, Plotinus seems to have felt compelled to reconcile his theory of the soul's descent with the idea of an orderly progression or emanation of being from a common source. His interpretation of the term *prothumia* as an expression of law might be viewed as a somewhat forced attempt to come to terms with the very fact of the soul's embodiment.[47]

Summation

In addressing the question of Soul's descent, Plotinus grappled with a problem that loomed large in Plato's philosophy. This problem concerns the disparity between the quasi-mythical fall account of the *Phaedrus* and the more optimistic picture of Soul's demiurgic role as presented in the *Timaeus*. While Plotinus attempts to resolve this problem, he never fully harmonizes the two theories.[48] As we have seen, the closest that he came to achieving something of a resolution is found in *Enneads* IV.8(6).5.3-8 and IV.3(27).13.7-22. In those passages, he connects the motive for Soul's descent with the operation of cosmic law. In the final analysis, he maintains an uneasy alliance between two positions: the one holds that souls are free, fallen, and culpable; the other that souls are determined, sent, and blameless.

The presence of *tolma* on the level of Soul creates the same tension that is evident on the level of *Nous*. As in the case of *Nous*, the tolmatic element cannot be divorced from Soul's downward movement. *Tolma* assumes increasing importance in regard to the emergence of the lower levels of reality, where differentiation and individuation is most pronounced. In some passages, Plotinus maintains that Soul's supervision of the material cosmos coincides with its contemplative activity. He occasionally identifies Soul's lower phase (i.e., the World Soul) with Nature, which bears the imprint of the intelligible world.

The World Soul functions as the *logos* of *Nous*, a rational principle which communicates form, intelligibility, and beauty to the material world.[49] Elsewhere, however, Plotinus assumes a more negative attitude toward the World Soul's focus upon lower levels of reality. *Ennead* III.7(45).11 designates this downward movement as the beginning of temporal process, a distention of Soul's powers upon a manifold of concerns. The same ambivalence is found in regard to the descent of individual souls toward matter.

Ennead V.1(10).1.1-10 attributes individual souls' descent to a number of motives. The primary motive is *tolma*, the audacity or assertiveness which Plotinus calls the beginning of evil for souls. But souls are also motivated by what he describes as a narcissistic egoism: the all-encompassing concern for the material cosmos is supplanted by a vain self-interest. In effect, souls desire more than they already possess; rather than participating in the supervision of the totality, they wish to embark on their own courses. In this respect, one finds an apparent affinity between *Enneads* III.7(45).11.15-23 and V.1(10).1.1-10. Both passages attribute the same motives to the lower phases of Soul: the desire for autonomy, self-determination, and the action, change, and differentiation characterizing temporal process.

While *Ennead* III.7(45).11.15-23 makes no explicit reference to *tolma*, it does discuss the operation of a "restlessly active nature" or "unquiet power" which displays a genuine kinship with the tolmatic surge. *Ennead* V.1(10).1.1-10 does refer to *tolma*, the primary motive for souls' descent. While the World Soul merely directs its attention to the temporal order, individual souls become directly involved with this ontological level of reality.

Plotinus's ambivalence toward Soul's descent is but a variation of the more fundamental tension evident in the emergence of *Nous*. Does otherness proceed as a result of the One's natural self-diffusiveness or does it emerge as the result of an illegitimate act of self-assertion (i.e., *tolma*)? In Plotinus, both explanations are upheld. The predominant, "majority opinion" of Plotinian treatises maintains that the lower levels of reality are good, beautiful, and intelligible. Nevertheless, Plotinus still remains attached to a pessimism in regard to plurality and otherness found in Gnostic, Hermeticist, and Neopythagorean writings. While the optimistic treatises may outweigh the pessimistic ones, Plotinus's ambivalence toward the material cosmos appears even in his most mature writings.

Notes

1. This point is made by A. H. Armstrong in a note at the beginning of his translation of *Ennead* V.1(10).1 (*Plotinus,* volume V in the *Loeb Classical Library* edition).

2. *Enneads* III.7(45).11.15-23; V.1(10).1.1-5.

3. *Ennead* V.1(10).5.1-2.

4. *Ennead* IV.2(1).(21).1.9-10; cf. *Ennead* VI.9(9).5.24-29.

5. *Ennead* V.2(11).1.16-28. In Plotinian terms, "Nature" encompasses the entire universe of being that is supervised by Soul, including the material cosmos as a whole, the celestial spheres, human existence, and animal and plant life.

6. Hans Jonas emphasizes Plotinus's use of the mythical motif in this passage and its affinities with Gnostic fall accounts ("The Soul in Gnosticism and Plotinus," *Le Néoplatonisme,* p. 52): "This is a mixture of ontology and drama, i.e., myth. The ontology articulates what time is in counterpart to eternity; the myth relates how time seceded from eternity. In doing so, the myth tells of forwardness and unrest, of an unquiet force, or unwillingness or inability to remain in concentrated wholeness, of a power that is thus at the same time a lack of power, of a desire to be self-subsistent and separate." Armstrong is more sceptical about a Gnostic influence ("Gnosis and Greek Philosophy," pp. 119-120), with the exception of the use of *tolma*-language.

7. *Ennead* III.7(45).11.9-14. cf. *Ennead* III.7(45).7.1-10.

8. *Ennead* III.7(45).5.18-30.

9. *Ennead* III.7(45).11.19-20. Armstrong translates the phrase "μῆκός τι τῆς πορείας ποιησάμενοι," as "we made a long stretch of our journey." But "πορείας" can also mean an act of walking or running or a course taken by a person (*Liddell and Scott,* p. 1254). This set of meanings seems closer to the spirit of the original text, since Plotinus is emphasizing that time involves an   arduous, step-by-step process. Such a fragmented mode of being stands in sharp contrast to eternity. In a footnote to the Greek text, Armstrong asserts that Plotinus's strange use of the third person

plural ("we made") might refer to Soul as individualized, and hence, a plurality of "souls."

10. *Ennead* III.8(30).8, 11.29-33.
Armstrong translates the phrase "πρῶτον μὲν ἑαυτὴν ἐχρόνωσεν" as "Soul . . . first of all put itself into time . . ." Hans Jonas renders the phrase in these terms: ". . . she first of all *temporalized herself* . . ." (in "The Soul in Gnosticism and Plotinus," p. 51). I have accepted Jonas's translation over that of Armstrong because, in my opinion, it appears to capture the true spirit of the original text. Jonas further offers (Ibid., p. 52) illuminating remarks regarding the verb-form "ἐχρόνωσεν" that Plotinus uses: "I know of no previous witness for the transitive verb *chronoo*; it is unique in Plotinus himself and probably coined by him to express a novel thought. Neither do I know of an after-history of the word. The coinage and its reflexive use bring out the difference from the Platonic model in the *Timaeus*. There, time is created; here, it is undergone by that which is going to create, as a self-alteration of its own being and a condition of its becoming creative." cf. *Ennead* III.7(45).11.29-35; 12.22-25.

11. *Ennead* III.7(45).11.59-12.4.

12. *Ennead* III.7(45).11.41-43.

13. *Liddell and Scott*, p. 1248. cf. the Latin counterpart *curiosus*.

14. Aristophanes, *Plutus* 913.

15. *Polybius* III, 38; V, 75; XI, 1.

16. Arrianus, *Discourses on Epictetus* III, 1, 21.

17. Plato, *Republic* VI.

18. Plato, *Republic* IV.

19. *Ennead* VI.7(38).36.1-15.

20. A similar use of the physical metaphor of "weight" is found in *Ennead* IV.3(27).15.1-7, where Plotinus discusses souls' gravitation toward material embodiment.

21. *Ennead* III.7 (45).11.20-33.

22. *Ennead* I.8(51).9.18-19: Διὸ καὶ νοῦς ἄλλος οὗτος, οὐ νοῦς, τολμήσας ἰδεῖν τὰ μὴ αὐτοῦ.

23. *Ennead* IV.8(6).2.26-38.

24. *Ennead* IV.3(27).9.29-39.

25. *Ennead* IV.8(6).2.1-14.   cf. *Enneads* IV.1(21).1.66-76; IV.3(27).4.31-33; 15.1-10.

26. *Ennead* IV.8(6) is closely related to *Ennead* V.1(10).1 in terms of its treatment of the soul's descent. In his notice to *Ennead* V.1, Brehier (Plotin, *Enneades* V, Paris, 1931, p. 8) cites the connection between the two works: "Le premier chapitre a été ecrit avec le souvenir récent des méditations sur la descente le l'âme dans le corps (le traité sur ce sujet, IV,8 est le sixième dans l'ordre chronologique, et le nôtre est le dixième: aussi commence-t-il par indiquer les raisons qui ont fait oublier a l'âme qu'elle a un dieu pour père."

27. *Ennead* V.1(10).1.1-10.

28. *Ennead* IV.8(6).4.10-12. cf. *Ennead* IV.8(6).7.1-14. The divine "father" to whom Plotinus refers in *Ennead* V.1(10).1.1-2 appears to be *Nous*, insofar as that principle, the basis of the intellectual cosmos, precedes Soul in the hierarchy of being.

29. *Ennead* IV.4(28).3.1-9.

30. *Ennead* IV.3(27).12.1-5.

31. *Ennead* V.2(11).2.1-10: ὅταν οὖν ψυχὴ ἐν φυτῷ γίνηται, ἄλλο ἐστὶν οἷον μέρος τὸ ἐν φυτῷ τὸ τολμηρότατον καὶ ἀφρονέστατον καὶ προεληλυθὸς μέχρι τοσούτου· ὅταν δ᾽ ἐν ἀλόγῳ, ἡ τοῦ αἰσθάνεσθαι δύναμις κρατήσασα ἤγαγεν·

32. *Ennead* I.8(51).9.18-26.

33. *Ennead* II.4(12).16.1-4.

34. An ongoing debate concerns Plotinus's attitude toward matter. Important studies on this topic are Edward B. Costello's "Is Plotinus Inconsistent on the Nature of Evil?" (*International Philosophical Quarterly* 7(1961): 483-497) and D.B. O'Brien's "Plotinus on Evil" (*Downside Review* LXXXVII (1969): 68-112). cf. *Ennead* I.8(51).5.1-19; II.4(12).16.1-4.

35. *Ennead* II.4(12).16.19-21.

36. A reference to the beggar-woman "Poverty" in Plato's myth of the birth of love (*Symposium* 203Bff.).

37. *Enneads* I.6(1).5.48-58.

38. *Ennead* I.8(51).14.44-49.

39. *Ennead* I.8(51).14.1-8. cf. *Ennead* I.6(1).5.25-31.

40. Plato, *Republic* IV (10, 11).

41. *Ennead* VI.4(22).15.23-32.

42. *Ennead* IV.4(28).21.4-6: . . . δῆλον γὰρ ὅτι τῷ σωματικὸν καὶ σῶμα τοιόνδε εἶναι πρεπόμενον παντοίας τροπὰς παντοδαπὰς καὶ τὰς ἐπιθυμίας ἴσχει . . .

43. *Ennead* IV.8(6).7.9-11: προθυμίᾳ δὲ πλείονι εἰς τὸ εἴσω δύοιτο μὴ μείνασα ὅλη μεθ᾽ ὅλης . . .

44. *Ennead* IV.3(27).13.27-32: ὠδῖνα ἐκεῖ ἐλθεῖν, οὐ ἐν αὐτοῖς ὢν οἷον ἐλθεῖν φθέγγεται.

45. According to *Ennead* V.2(11).1.22-28, even the higher part of Soul displays a tendency to generate inferior levels of reality: διὸ καὶ δοκεῖ καὶ ἡ ἄνω ψυχὴ μέχρι φυτῶν φθάνειν· τρόπον γάρ τινα φθάνει, ὅτι αὐτῆς τὸ ἐν φυτοῖς· οὐ μὴν πᾶσα ἐν φυτοῖς, ἀλλὰ γιγνομένη ἐν φυτοῖς οὕτως ἐστίν, ὅτι ἐπὶ τοσοῦτον προέβη εἰς τὸ κατω ὑπόστασιν ἄλλην ποιησαμένη τῇ προόδῳ καὶ προθυμίᾳ τοῦ χείρονος.

46. *Ennead* IV.8(6).5.10-14; 24-27.

47. One finds a similar tension in the early writings of St. Augustine, who also seemed to struggle to reconcile the soul's fall with the dictates of a higher law (e.g. *De Genesi contra Manichaeos* II, 22). Like Plotinus, he viewed the soul as both "fallen" and "sent" to order the body.

48. Plotinus refers to these conflicting Platonic accounts in *Ennead* IV.8(6).1.23-50. This tension has been recognized by various scholars. Brehier (*The Philosophy of Plotinus*, trans. Joseph Thomas (Chicago: University of Chicago Press, 1971) p. 72), writes in terms of an "undeniable contradiction" between these two accounts. Inge (*The Philosophy of Plotinus*, volume I (London: Longmans, Green and Co., 1923), p. 259) describes "a want of firmness in this part of his philosophy."

49. *Ennead* III.8(30).5.10-14. cf. *Enneads* III.2(47).16.10-17.

Chapter V

The Significance of Plotinian *Tolma*

The preceding chapters have demonstrated that *tolma* assumes a key role in Plotinus's metaphysical scheme, providing the impetus to differentiation on all levels of the intelligible universe. On the basis of this analysis, it is apparent that the issue of *tolma's* role in the *Enneads* is intimately connected with a nettling problem in Plotinian philosophy regarding the very presence of otherness (i.e., anything other than the One). Otherness and plurality pose a major stumbling block for Plotinus, since anything other than the One must be less than this supreme reality in goodness, life, and power. The ontological "distance" between the One's primal unity and its effects necessitates some principle of differentiation.

This brings to the fore what can be characterized as the "problem of otherness" in the *Enneads*, an issue which might be analyzed in terms of two questions. First, why does anything other than the One exist, since otherness provides the basis of imperfection, deficiency, and evil in Plotinus's metaphysical scheme? Secondly, how is the manifold derived from the One? Stating the question in different terms, how do we bridge the gap between the One and the diversity which characterizes the lower levels of reality? Plotinus's attempts to respond to these questions give rise to an unresolved tension in his system between optimistic and pessimistic interpretations regarding the emergence of anything other than the One.

In Plotinian terms, the rationale for the One's emanation is found in the necessity of its outpouring: because the One is essentially good, and because goodness must communicate itself, the One is naturally self-diffusive. The manifold represents the effect or consequence of the One's own emanation. But in addressing the question of the derivation of the manifold from the One, Plotinus suggests that the movement toward otherness (and hence, toward non-being) is somehow rooted in the One's creative outpouring itself. This movement (in both Nous and Soul) assumes the character of a will toward separate, autonomous existence.

The Plotinian Tension

The *Enneads* thus present the reader with two explanations for the transition from absolute unity to multiplicity: (1) an optimistic emanation/diffusion account, stressing the natural outpouring of the One's goodness; and (2) several pessimistic accounts, emphasizing the will to otherness that manifests itself as *tolma*. According to the first type of account, emanation is the necessary, spontaneous expression of the One's essential goodness, which must communicate itself. According to the second type of account, emanation coincides with a volitional fall.

The presence of such disparate accounts gives rise to something of a faultline in the *Enneads*, the result of an uneasy alliance between a positive outlook regarding the emergence of plurality, and a pessimistic fall motif, reminiscent of Gnostic as well as Neopythagorean and Hermeticist speculation. Although Plotinus stresses the orderly progresssion of all things from the One, he inserts an irrational element of *tolma* into his otherwise highly rationalistic metaphysics. In addition to his emphasis upon the goodness of emanation and its effects, he presents the alternate thesis that otherness is wrong and that its emergence proceeds from a culpable act of will. Such applications of *tolma*-language to the descending movement of being bespeaks a conflict which permeates Plotinus's entire metaphysics.

Such "negative" will (that is, a will directed away from the One) first arises in *Nous*, the initial instance of being in the intelligible universe. In some passages, as we have seen, Plotinus describes *Nous's* emergence in extremely positive terms: *Nous* is closely in touch with the One as the recipient of its power, goodness, and life; by virtue of its contemplation of the One, *Nous* becomes the repository of Forms, the intelligible expressions of the One's boundless energy (*Enneads* V.2(11).1.9-13; V.3(49).11.1-10; VI.7(38).15.10-14). But Plotinus also describes

Nous's emergence in terms of a voluntary descent (*Ennead* VI.9(9).5.24-29;   III.8(30).8.31-38;   V.8(31).13.1-11).   *Ennead* V.1(10).7.13-17 discusses the ambiguity inherent in *Nous's* emergence, stressing that while it stands as the very image of the One and the product of its outpouring, it also acts on its own account.

One finds a similar tension on the level of Soul. As in Plotinus's approach to matter, we find him struggling with a problem inherited from Plato in his deliberations upon the descent of Soul. This problem grows out of the conflicting accounts found in the *Phaedrus* and *Timaeus* regarding the Soul's relation to matter. The presence of opposing interpretations of Soul's descent (through one of its lower phases) in the *Enneads* gives rise to what Emile Bréhier defined as that "undeniable contradiction" in Plotinian emanation theory.[1] In various places, Plotinus applauds Soul's presence to Nature and the material cosmos (*Ennead* V.2(11).1.16-22). Just as *Nous* is closely aligned with the One, Soul displays a kinship with the contemplative life of *Nous* (e.g. *Ennead* V.9(5).3.24-37), holding a mid-rank between the Intellectual-Principle and the lower orders of reality (*Ennead* IV.6(41).3.10-12). From this optimistic standpoint, the material cosmos is the product of Soul's contemplative activity and the recipient of intelligibility, Form, and order (*Enneads* IV.3(27).14.1-5).

But this positive conception of Soul's downward tendency is offset by a more negative interpretation which views it in rather disparaging terms. In this respect, Soul's governance of Nature either results in a distention of its powers (*Ennead* III.7 (45).11.15-23) or plunges it into a narrow, self-centered mode of existence (*Ennead* IV.8(6).4.10-21). Soul's *tolma* generates temporal process and precipitates the embodiment of material things (*Enneads* V.1(10).1.1-10; V.2(11).2.1-10; III.7(45).11.15-23). But while *Nous's tolma* culminates in an eternal contemplation of the One, the *tolma* of Soul directs it toward unstable reality (i.e., Nature and matter). In response to *tolma*, lower phases of Soul eschew the stability of noetic contemplation for the novelty and change inherent in temporality. Once bound to bodies, individual souls rely upon images for their knowledge and engage in the painstaking process of discursive reasoning from premises to conclusions.

According to such accounts, the descent of souls into matter proceeds from a deeply rooted desire for self-assertion, autonomy, and change. In the context of Plotinus's metaphysics, such a yearning can only have negative effects. Once estranged from the stability of the contemplative life of *Nous*, souls subject themselves to the vicissitudes and limitations of human existence. Soul's *tolma* constitutes a kind of renegade individualism which runs counter to the life of participation in the supervision of the entire cosmos as exercised by the World Soul.

Tolma and the Metaphysics of Volition

But the tensions that we encounter in Plotinus's *Enneads* reflect a larger tension in the history of western metaphysics between two distinct visions of reality. One vision defines the really real in terms of oneness and stability, the other in terms of multiplicity and change. Plotinus is representative of the first viewpoint, standing in continuity with the rationalism of Parmenides, the Eleatics, and Plato. As a thoroughgoing rationalist in his own right, Plotinus attempted to derive all things from a single metaphysical principle. But this monistic bent resulted in a devaluation of the world of sense experience, along with its plurality and diversity.

As we have seen, Plotinus retained vestiges of a pessmistic outlook concerning the emergence of reality which stands in sharp contrast with the more dominant optimism of his philosophy. This pessimism finds expression in those passages which employ *tolma* or closely related language in explaining the generation of *Nous*, Soul, and Soul's lower phases. On these various levels, *tolma* manifests itself as a will toward separate existence. In effect, Plotinus inserts will into the emanation process itself, presenting what has been characterized as a "metaphysics of volition," running parallel to those accounts that stress the rational deduction of the manifold from the One.[2] By introducing an affective element into the emanation process, Plotinus provided an interesting metaphysical innovation. For him, will is instrumental in the descending movement of being from the

One. Such will, that is, *boulēsis* (βούλεσις) is present on every level of the intelligible universe.

The *Boulēsis* of the One

Plotinus attributes an element of *boulēsis* to the One itself. The fullest discussion of this primal will is found in *Ennead* VI.8(39), which defines the very nature of the One in terms of will:

> For if we should impart operations to him, and his operations to what is like his will—for he does not operate without willing—and the operations are like his substance, his will and substance are the same. And if this is the case, then as he willed, in this manner he is. Then he does not will and operate as it is his nature to do, any more than his substance is as he wills and operates.[3]

But, he informs us, such a distinction between the One and its activities (which might suggest a duality in the One's own nature) is made for the sake of verbal expediency alone. For this reason, Plotinus urges a patience with language, speaking in figurative rather than in literal terms.[4] From our limited perspective, any idea of the One demands that we include in it the *boulēsis* which constitutes its being. If the One is to be viewed as a distinct reality in its own right, it must will its being and conversely, be what it wills. In this sense, the One maintains itself by means of will.

Boulēsis, then, seems to provide a necessary condition for the One's existence. Since the One is a monadic unity (a unified, self-contained whole admitting of neither duality nor distinction of any kind), its will and its being must be identical. In this respect, the One's *boulēsis* carries this implication: the One also wills to be what it is.[5] This choice, however, cannot be a truly free one; because the One is the Supreme Good, it could be nothing other than what it is. Its will coincides with the best of all possible realities.[6] By attributing this element of choice to the One's own constitution, Plotinus wishes to uphold its freedom from determination by any external sources. As its own cause, the One is immune to the influences of chance and blind necessity. In this respect, the One is not what it happens to be, but what it wills to be.

As already demonstrated, Plotinus accounts for the derivation of the manifold from the One by means of the One's own self-diffusiveness. For the One is not only its own cause; it is the cause of everything in the universe of being, that is, everything which follows it in reality. Everything depends upon this supreme principle for its existence. But the One's creative out-pouring can only be described in metaphorical terms. In other treatises, Plotinus resorts to such images as the radiation of light from a common source (*Enneads* V.3(49).12.39-44; 17.33-37) or the flowing of water from a spring or fountain (*Ennead* III.8(30).10.3-10) to explicate this movement. In *Ennead* VI.8, however, he draws directly upon human experience, describing this diffusion in terms of love, or more precisely, in terms of a self-directed love which is inseparable from the One's own nature.[7] Because the One is absolutely perfect, it can only love itself; any inclination toward something external would threaten the One's unity. But in loving itself, the One generates Nous and consequently, provides the basis of the intelligible patterns of all things.[8]

Boulēsis, Tolma, and Descent

On its highest level, *boulēsis* is intimately connected with the One's causal activity. The One's will-to-be, a will that is self-directed, overflows as a diffusive love. Because the object of the One's will is supremely good, the will that seeks that object is also good. But on lower hypostatic levels (i.e., that of *Nous* and Soul), will can only be directed toward something other than the One.

From a Neoplatonic standpoint, that which is other than the One must be imperfect and ontologically inferior. Conse-quently, the *boulēsis* of *Nous* and Soul (as well as that of Soul's lower phases) constitutes a blameworthy desire. Whereas the One's *boulēsis* was directed toward primal unity, the *boulesis* exhibited by these lower hypostases seeks increasing degrees of differentiation and autonomy. In this sense, the will-to-be of *Nous* and Soul represents an irrational drive away from the One, and hence, a movement toward non-being and privation. Thus, the entire mechanism of descent presupposes a willful desire for otherness.

We see, then, a transformation in Plotinus's attitude toward *boulēsis* when it is considered on levels other than the One. There, such will expresses itself as *tolma*, the desire for otherness which Plotinus views as blameworthy. The clearest indication of this volitional movement on the part of *Nous* is found in *Ennead* VI.9(9).5.24-29. But a tension emerges in that discussion as a result of two conflicting desires. Plotinus maintains that the first principle desires or wants to be one (ἓν μὲν εἶναι βουλομένου) but it is not one (οὐκ ὄντος δὲ ἕν). The One's apparently unfulfilled desire for unity coincides with a daring or audacity in *Nous* to "stand apart" from the One: ". . . so near to the One, yet *somehow* it desired to stand apart with audacity" (ἀποστῆναι δέ πως ἑνὸς τολμήσας).

In this passage, Plotinus seems to struggle with the fact of otherness and its attendant plurality and diversity of being. From Plotinus's monistic standpoint, unity must be preferable to multiplicity. Nonetheless, the One's desire (that is, to be one) seems unrealized. Further, while *Nous* is near to the One (and almost indistinguishable from its source), its very being presupposes a will toward otherness that separates it from that higher principle. At the base of this "standing apart" is *tolma*, an expression of will that is constitutive of *Nous* in two ways: first, as that which prompts the emergence of something other than the One; secondly, as that which sustains *Nous* as a distinct hypostasis.

In epistemological terms, the comprehension of truth and being diminishes in proportion to its degree of ontological distance from the One. On the level of *Nous*, *tolma* initiates and sustains this first instance of being. But, insofar as knowledge demands a dichotomy between knower and that which is known, *tolma* allows for the possibility of knowledge within the Plotinian scheme. Since *tolma* prompts the emergence of something other than the One, it opens up the epistemological distinction between *Nous* (as eternal contemplator of the One) and the One itself (the highest object of contemplation). By virtue of its eternal contemplation of the One, *Nous* translates the One's unlimited power into the world of intelligible Forms. In effect,

Plotinus formulated an alternate account of *Nous's* emergence which clashes with his more prominent rationalistic deduction of all things from the One. This alternate account reflects the Neopythagorean dimension of his thought, wherein the generation of plurality is viewed in negative terms.

As I have demonstrated, a key historical source of Plotinian *tolma* lies in the Neopythagorean tradition of Middle Platonism. The Neopythagorean equation of the *Dyad* with *tolma* was a highly significant development, insofar as it established a connection between *tolma* and the emergence of plurality. Moreover, the conceptual merger of the two terms imparted the status of evil to multiplicity and otherness. In this respect, evil was interpreted in terms of an estrangement from a monadic unity. Thus, the very appearance of the *Dyad* was viewed as wrong. This pessimism toward the manifold was carried over into the philosophy of Plotinus. Like his Neopythagorean predecessors and contemporaries, he relegated multiplicity to an inferior status in the hierarchy of being. His applications of *tolma*-language to the descent of Nous thus points to a Neopythagorean influence upon his thinking.

Tolma's manifestation on the level of *Nous* provides the basis of a general tendency toward otherness, multiplicity, and individuation. On lower levels, *tolma* prompts Soul's distention from its timeless, self-contained noetic contemplation (*Ennead* III.7(45).11.15-23).[9] As in the case of *Nous*, phases of the third hypostasis are guilty of overstepping their proper boundaries or overextending themselves beyond their proper spheres. Soul's movement, like that of *Nous* is described in terms of a rebelliousness or apostasy (*Enneads* IV.2(1).(21).1.9-10; V.1(10).5.1-2). For *Nous*, this apostasy or "standing apart" (ἀποστῆναι) proceeds from its desire "to possess all things."[10] In Soul, the fault lies in a drive that is directed toward self-determination and autonomy (*Enneads* V.1(10).1.1-10; IV.8(6).4.10-12; IV.4(28).3.1-9), or in a desire to engage in independent activity, apart from full participation in a higher contemplative life (*Ennead* IV.8(6).2.26-38; IV.7(2).13.1-13).

In this context, Plotinus's uses of *tolma*-language display some interesting filiations with the *tolma* of Gnosticism and the *Hermetica*, where it was interpreted as a kind of "root fault," that is, a rash audacity or arrogance which provides the motive for a decline from a higher to a lower metaphysical plane. In those systems, *tolma* also expressed a desire for self-determination, usually manifesting itself in the vain attempt to undertake an imitative creation. In a similar manner, as we have seen, Judeo-Christian writers of the Alexandrian milieu (e.g. Philo Judaeus and Clement) discussed *tolma* in terms of the Scriptural sin of idolatry or an insolent curiosity for knowledge of those matters reserved for God alone.

A consideration of the role of *tolma* on the part of Soul should begin with *Ennead* III.7(45).11.15-23, the passage wherein Plotinus discusses the distention of the World Soul in time. Although he does not explicitly apply *tolma*-language to Soul in this context, its meaning seems implicit throughout the passage: Plotinus inserts an element of *boulēsis* into the life of Soul which directs it downward, and hence, away from *Nous* and the life of noetic contemplation. Plotinus, as we have seen, attributes this downward inclination to a restless nature which sought self-determination and autonomy.

But to what extent can this "restless nature" be viewed as a species of *tolma* ? While such a question does not admit of any conclusive responses, it would appear that the "polupragmatic" Soul discussed in *Ennead* III.7(45).11.15-23 exhibits characteristics similar to those of individual souls driven by *tolma*. *Ennead* V.1(10).1.1-10, attributes the descent of souls to four factors: (1) an act of self-will or *tolma*; (2) the desire for self-ownership or self-determination; (3) a desire for differentiation; and (4) the entry into the sphere of temporal process. In this respect, an extremely close relationship is evident between *Enneads* III.7(45).11.15-23 and V.1(10).1.1-10. In both passages, the initiation of temporal process (and the very involvement with temporality) is viewed in terms of a declension.

In strict Plotinian terms, the hypostasis Soul neither falls into time nor descends into material bodies. Rather, *Ennead* III.7(45).11.15-23 describes the process whereby Soul focuses downward in supervising lower ontological levels. Unlike individual souls (which are directly involved with the bodies they govern and animate), Soul always remains aloof, supervising the cosmos as a whole from a distance. Nevertheless, the clear

affinities between *Enneads* III.7(45).11.15-23 and V.1(10).1.1-10
justifies a linking of Soul's temporalization with Plotinus's
theory of souls' descent into matter. [11]

In these discussions, Plotinus emphasizes the volitional character of descent. This volitional character is reflected in his
application of *boulēsis* (and its verb-forms) as well as the verb
ethelo (ἐθέλω) to the downward movement of the different
phases of Soul. Both *boulēsis* and *ethelō* express the ideas of
desire, wish, or more precisely, a willingness or deliberateness.
The blameworthiness of Soul's (or souls') deviation proceeds
from that volitional element embedded within its own nature.
When used in conjunction with *tolma* (or related language),
such terminology connotes a tragic flaw or a kind of "original
sin' which precipitates the beginning of evil or opens the possibility of moral error by virtue of Soul's attachment to material
bodies.[12]   In this respect, Plotinus distinguishes between the
descent of souls and the moral wrongs committed once they are
embodied.[13] If it were not for their descent, souls would never
be subjected to the influences of the body which prompt them
to forget their true spiritual origins.

But, as we have seen, the later Plotinus maintains that the
choice for descent is not completely free: souls choose to
descend in response to the dictates of a higher law. Here, volition coincides with cosmic necessity. In effect, the reader of the
Enneads is confronted with several distinct accounts of the
descent of souls: an optimistic emanation/diffusion account
and the various pessimistic ones which either specify an act of
tolma, prothumia, or other motives (i.e., self-love or narcissism;
concupiscence or *epithumia*).

When Plotinus designates *prothumia* as an expression of cosmic necessity, his intention is apparent: he wishes to somehow
explain why souls would abandon their status as participants in
the totality of Soul in favor of the vicissitudes of human existence. Plotinus's diverse attempts to rationalize this fact suggest
that he was groping for a solution to a nettling problem that
eluded him. Accordingly, we are left with an unresolved tension
in his philosophy, which advances the alternate theses that the
soul is both "fallen" and "sent" to govern the body.

Concluding Remarks

On purely metaphysical grounds, it would appear that Plotinus's system requires a principle of differentiation such as *tolma* which both prompts and sustains reality other than the One. This is especially evident on the level of *Nous*, the first instance of otherness within the intelligible universe. Plotinus might have addressed the question of being's emergence solely on the basis of his account of the One's emanation or diffusion of its own goodness. However, the very presence of pessimistic fall accounts paralleling his emanation/diffusion account suggests an ongoing struggle with a number of difficulties inherent in his metaphysics.

To begin, it would appear that Plotinus could not fully explain the emergence of being on the basis of an emanation/diffusion account alone. Why, indeed, would the One diffuse itself into lower, imperfect levels of reality? Secondly, the emanation/diffusion account does not adequately explain how that which is infinite, unlimited, and unbounded gives rise to that which is finite, limited, and circumscribed. How, in effect, does it bridge the ontological gap between its own supreme power and that which follows after it? Third, the fact of evil in the cosmos creates a problem for a metaphysics that grounds itself upon a supremely perfect first principle. How do we account for the presence of evil in the world if all things are the products of the One's creative outpouring?

Such difficulties seem to have led Plotinus to formulate an alternate series of accounts which impute reality other than the One to a tragic flaw. In these accounts, he came to terms with the fact of impefection by attributing the cause of lower reality to some kind of "original sin" which disrupted the self-contained stability of the One. From this pessimistic standpoint, reality other than the One should have never emerged.

Indeed, the entire Plotinian mechanism of descent presupposes a willful desire for otherness, separation, and autonomy. In regard to the notion of will itself, Plotinus presents us with an important innovation. In the *Enneads*, will assumes a prominent metaphysical role as a dynamic component in the procession of being from the One. This will toward otherness is instrumental in the emergence of the lower hypostases of *Nous* and Soul, as well as in the embodiment of individual souls. Paradoxically, the One is somehow ultimately responsible for the surge toward multiplicity.

Notes

1. Emile Brehier, *The Philosophy of Plotinus*, trans. Joseph Thomas (Chicago: University of Chicago Press, 1971), p. 72.

2. Vernon Bourke characterizes Plotinian metaphysics in these terms in his illuminating work *Will In Western Thought* (New York, 1964), p. 18.

3. *Ennead* VI.8(39).5-9.

4. *Ennead* VI.8(39).13.1-5; 47-50.

5. *Ennead* VI.8(39).13.58-59: οὐχ ὅπερ ᾽ἔτυχεν ἐστιν, ἀλλ᾽ὅπερ ἐβουλήθη αὐτός.

6. *Ennead* VI.8(39).13.38-40: ῎Εστι γὰρ ὄντως ἡ ἀγαθοῦ φύσις θέλησις αὐτοῦ οὐ δεδεκασμένου οὐδε τῇ ἑαυτοῦ φύσει ἐπισπωμένου, ἀλλ᾽ ἑαυτὸν, ἑλομένου, ὅτι μηδὲ ἦν ἄλλο,᾽ἵνα πρὸς ἐκεῖνο ἐλχθῇ.

7. *Ennead* VI.8(39).15.1-2;8-10: καὶ ἐράσμιον καὶ ἔρως ὁ αὐτος καὶ αὐτοῦ ἔρως, ᾽ἅτε οὐκ ᾽ἄλλως καλὸς ᾽ἢ παρ᾽αὐτοῦ καὶ ἐν αὐτῷ . . . εἰ δὲ τοῦτο, πάλιν αὖ αὐτός ἐστιν οὗτος ὁ ποιῶν ἑαυτὸν καὶ κύριος ἑαυτοῦ καὶ οὐχ ὥς τι ἕτερον ἠθέλησε γενόμενος, ἀλλ᾽ὡς θέλει αὐτός.

8. *Ennead* VI.8(39).18.38-41.

9. In Soul, the fault lies in a drive that is directed toward self-determination and autonomy (*Enneads* V.1(10).1.1-10; V.1(10).5,1-2; IV.8(6).4.10-12) or in a desire for an individualized mode of existence (*Ennead* IV.4(28).3.1-9).

10. *Ennead* III.8(30).8.31-38.

11. Although *Ennead* III.7(45).11.15-23 contains no explicit reference to *tolma*, it discusses Soul's defection from the life of *Nous* in a manner closely akin to the fall account of *Ennead* V.1(10).1.1-10 in a number of ways. First, *Ennead* III.7(45).11.15-16 stresses the desire for self-determination (καὶ ᾽ἄρχειν αὐτῆς βουλομένης καὶ εἶναι αὐτῆς) as a prime motive for Soul's defection from *Nous; Ennead* V.1(10).1.5 likewise cites the "desire for self-ownership" (βουλήθηναι δὲ ἑαυτῶν εἶναι) as a motive for the descent of individual souls. Secondly, *Ennead* III.7(45).11.29-30 delineates the movement whereby Soul temporalizes itself and fashions

time in imitation of eternity; so too, *Ennead* V.1(10).1.4 designates temporal involvement or the "entry into the sphere of process" (ἡγένεσις) as a source of the evil befalling individual souls. Thirdly, *Ennead* III.7(45).11.19-20 characterizes Soul's movement as a distention of its powers in the temporal manifold; *Ennead* V.l(10).1.1-7 similarly attributes the descent of souls to a desire for movement for the sake of movement, a desire which puts them on the wrong course.

12. *Ennead* V.1(10).1.1-10. cf. *Ennead* V.1(10).5.1-2: τῇ δὲ ὑπάρχειεν ἐν τούτοις εἶναι συνφείσῃ, εἰ μὴ ἀποστατεῖν ἐθέλοι. *Ennead* IV.4(28).3.2: καὶ ἕτερον ἐθελήσασα εἶναι . . .

13. *Ennead* IV.8(6).5.16-18: Διττῆς δὲ τῆς ἁμαρτίας οὔσης, τῆς μὲν ἐπὶ τῇ τοῦ κατελθεῖν αἰτίᾳ, τῆς δὲ ἐπὶ τῷ ἐνθάδε γενομένην κακὰ δρᾶσαι . . .

Chapter VI

Plotinus's Intellectual Evolution
And Its Implications

In the face of a number of apparent inconsistencies in Plotinus's account of the emergence of reality other than the One, we must consider a possible development of thought in the *Enneads*. The question of an evolution in Plotinus's thinking is particularly relevant in respect to accounts of the descent of the lower phases of Soul. As we have seen, Plotinus attributes the motive for the descent of psychic principles to *tolma*. In the absence of *tolma*-language, we encounter a number of passages which imply that the descent of souls is the result of some illegitimate act of self-assertion. But elsewhere, Plotinus approaches the descent of souls in terms of a response to the demands of cosmic law. According to this latter theory, the association of souls with material bodies is viewed as necessary for the completion and formation of the material universe.

But in this context, a problem immediately presents itself when one considers Plotinus's use of *tolma*, since that term also assumed some importance in the speculative systems of the Gnostics. Yet, despite his clear anti-Gnostic stance, Plotinus resorted to the terminology of those very Gnostic systems in various accounts of the descent of being. The application of *tolma*-language in describing the differentiation of both the second and third hypostases (*Nous* and Soul, respectively) carries some apparent Gnostic overtones. As Hans Jonas has observed, "the language turns from philosophical to mythological and, with all his distaste for gnostic 'tragedy-mongering,' comes dangerously close to gnostic mythologizing."[1] Jonas's observation directs us to the intriguing and much debated issue concerning the possible presence of a Gnostic element in the *Enneads*. Before addressing this issue, let us consider the mainlines of

Plotinus's extended anti-Gnostic polemic and the reference to *tolma*-language that emerges in that context.

Plotinus's Anti-Gnostic Polemic

Plotinus's most glaring critique of the Gnostics is found in *Ennead* II.9 (thirty-third treatise in Porphyry's chronological ordering). But *Ennead* II.9 must be considered as the culmination of a longer work that is divided and grouped in four consecutive treatises numbered thirty, thirty-one, thirty-two, and thirty-three, respectively: *Ennead* III.8 (*"On Nature and Contemplation"*), *Ennead* V.8 (*"On the Intelligible Beauty"*), *Ennead* V.5 (*"That The Intelligibles Are Not Outside Intellect And The Good"*), and finally, *Ennead* II.9 (*"Against The Gnostics "*).

While these treatises are very rich in content, the present survey will provide but a general overview of key themes. Rather than attempting to engage in an in-depth analysis of these writings, I will merely consider some of their more salient features: the emphasis upon the unity of reality as a whole and the affirmation of the continuity (rather than the discontinuity and separateness) between the various levels of reality.

In *Ennead* III.8(30).1, Plotinus articulates the principle that all action and productivity is directed toward contemplation.[2] Reality is identified with thought, and productivity with thinking or more precisely, with contemplation. Rather than focusing upon a tolmatic desire on Nous's part for autonomy (as he did in *Ennead* VI.9(9).5.24-29), Plotinus now highlights the rational, orderly progression of all things from the One by virtue of an intellectual vision of the Good. Here, contemplation is related to productivity and generation, just as *tolma* is related to otherness. Thus, the One's self-contemplation of its own essential goodness generates *Nous* (the first instance of otherness), *Nous's* contemplation of the One generates Soul, and Soul's contemplation of *Nous* gives rise to Nature and ultimately, the material cosmos.

In Plotinian terms, the universe is maintained by form from beginning to end. Even matter, lying at the farthest reaches of the intelligible universe, is determined by the form of the elements.[3] In this regard, natural beauty and cosmic order must originate in the intelligible world, deriving their form from that higher realm. For Plotinus, the artist (as one who produces beautiful things) has direct access to the intelligibility of *Nous* and its Forms.[4] In broader cosmic terms, Plotinus maintains that Nature's rational forming principle cannot originate in Nature itself. Rather, it is *Nous* which shapes the cosmos without any planning or deliberation. For Plotinus, the spontaneity and ease with which *Nous* engages in contemplative production demonstrates that genuine thought is always of a non-discursive character.[5] In effect, *Nous* is depicted as existing in union with its intelligible objects, the Forms or patterns of things which Plotinus views as living realities in their own right, rather than theoretical, abstract concepts.[6]

These deliberations culminate in *Ennead* II.9(33), where Plotinus attempts to refute Gnostic teachings on a variety of subjects while supporting classical doctrines regarding the nature of truth, knowledge and the emergence of the material universe. At the outset, he upholds a triadic model of hypostases against those who would attempt to multiply intelligible realities (especially *Nous*) or to make unwarranted distinctions between these principles.[7] He next presents what he considers the true doctrine of Soul, maintaining that Soul as an entirety cannot descend.[8] In this respect, he opposes the Gnostic belief in an abrupt, cataclysmic break in the hierarchy of being, an event which according to their interpretation, resulted in the creation of the world. From a Plotinian perspective, all things must, of necessity, exist forever in an orderly dependence upon one another. All realities other than the One are derived from higher principles. These insights lay the groundwork for Plotinus's polemic against the Gnostic notion that the material universe is the product of an error or sin and the accompanying pessimism toward the cosmos that such a teaching engendered.

Referring to Plato's *Phaedrus* (246C) and its characterization of Soul as "shedding its wings," Plotinus denies that the cosmos proceeds from the descent of All-Soul.[9] Implicit in this teaching is the Gnostics' arrogance in believing that they possess true knowledge of the very nature of things. But it also bespeaks a tendency to apply conclusions drawn from human experience to the spiritual order. This would be comparable, Plotinus suggests, to indicting a well-ordered city on the basis of the shoddy work of its potters or smiths.[10]

Plotinus next addresses the question as to why Soul fashioned the universe. This question, he maintains, is put by those who assume that the universe must have a temporal beginning.[11] In opposition to this teaching, Plotinus upholds the eternal character of the universe and the spontaneity of its production without any planning on the part of its maker. This contention points the way to a critique of the Gnostic myth of the fall of *Sophia* (*Ennead* II.9(33), *chapters* 10-12), the portion of the treatise that is of primary importance for the present considerations.[12]

Plotinus characterizes the myth as that which exceeds all of their doctrines in absurdity.[13] This point concerns the teaching that Soul, along with "Wisdom" or *Sophia*, declined and in so doing, brought down individual souls with it to inhabit material bodies. According to the account in question, Soul descends to the lowest level of reality, the realm of images. As discussed in Chapter I, Irenaeus's famous account of the myth (*Adversus Haereses* I) depicts *Sophia* as attempting to comprehend the mystery of the Godhead. This rash desire, which he identifies as *tolma*, prompted her fall, the act whereby the universe was produced. In his anti-Gnostic polemic, Plotinus reacts against the suggestion that the cosmos is the product of a transgression or "original sin" of some kind. "How," he queries, "will their statements still apply that it created for the sake of being honoured, and how does it create out of arrogance and . . . self-assertion (that is, *tolma*)?"[14]

A Rejection of *Tolma*-Language?

In effect, Plotinus attributes the use of *tolma*-language directly to his Gnostic adversaries, in the context of their discussions of the creation of the material world. Dodds invested this particular assertion with much importance, viewing it as something of a transitional point in Plotinus's thinking:

> A change comes when he breaks finally with Gnosticism. In the essay *Against the Gnostics* it is his opponents who think that the soul created

the world 'out of arrogance and *tolma*.' Henceforth the *tolma*-language is dropped from his own teaching, and the descent even of the individual soul is no longer viewed as a sin. [15]

Dodds' observation brings to the fore what has been characterized as a "shift in accent" in Plotinus's outlook. [16] According to this thesis, Plotinus's thought underwent a marked transformation after his extended polemic against the Gnostics. From this standpoint, his opposition to extreme forms of Gnostic dualism coincided with a more pronounced optimism toward Nature and the material cosmos as a whole that was consistent with Platonic and Stoic teachings, and in wider terms, with the Greek rationalist tradition in general.

But if Dodds contention is an accurate one, then the role and sigificance of *tolma* in the *Enneads* becomes, for all practical purposes, a dead issue. Where it does appear, such terminology might merely reflect an earlier stage of Plotinus's intellectual development when (in Armstrong's assessment) Plotinus "had himself . . . been prepared to make some concessions" to views espoused by Gnostics or by gnosticizing Platonists. [17]   In that case, however, the pessimistic side of Plotinian thought which I have delineated thus far could likewise be viewed as but a passing phase that was eventually supplanted by an optimistic outlook.

But did Plotinus exhibit a genuine "shift in accent" after his anti-Gnostic polemic, and if so, how great a transformation did his thought undergo in the process? In this regard, John Rist charges that Dodds "seems to overestimate the change in Plotinus's doctrines caused by his open rupture with Gnosticism. [18] This charge proceeds from the assumption that when Plotinus criticized the Gnostics (in *Ennead* II.9(33).11.19-22) for viewing the world as the product of·Soul's "arrogance and rash self-assertion," it was the World Soul that he had in mind and not the individual soul. Rist stresses that Plotinus used *tolma*-language only when speaking about the descent of individual souls. [19]   From this standpoint, his opposition to the Gnostics was based upon their use of *tolma*-language in describing the motive for the World Soul's creative activity.

But while Rist's contention that Dodds "overestimates" the change in Plotinus's teachings is a valid one, I think that his explanation of Plotinus's use of *tolma*-language is a bit narrow. To begin with, his distinction between the activity of the World Soul and the descent of individual souls implies that these movements constitute two separate developments. But, as I have demonstrated, the descent of individual souls might be viewed as part of a general defection on the part of Soul from the life of *Nous* and the gravitation toward temporality that Plotinus discusses in *Ennead* III.7(45).11.15-23. Thus, there seems to be a much closer connection between Plotinus's account of Soul's temporalization in *Ennead* III.7(45).11 and the account of souls' descent into matter in *Enneads* V.1(10).1.1-10 and V.2(11).1.1-10 than Rist's interpretation would allow.

Furthermore, several passages in the *Enneads* suggest an element of *tolma* in Plotinus's scheme on levels higher than that occupied by individual souls. Indeed, the language of *Ennead* III.7(45).11.15-23 (written well after the anti-Gnostic polemic) can easily call to mind some of the fall accounts prominent in Gnosticism, Neopythagoreanism, and the *Hermetica*. And although Plotinus does not explicitly use *tolma*-language in that passage, his references to Soul's "restlessly active nature" and to its "unquiet power" are strongly suggestive of the sort of root fault or transgression that *tolma* designates elsewhere in his writings. As we shall see, Plotinus's later pronouncements could be as pessimistic toward reality other than the One as his early ones (even in the absence of *tolma*-language).

Of course, an effective response to Dodds would be evidence of the presence of *tolma*-language later than *Ennead* II.9(33). For what it is worth, such language does, in fact, appear in *Ennead* VI.7 (thirty-eighth treatise in chronological order—apparently composed well after the anti-Gnostic treatises). In *Ennead* VI.7(38).31, we find the same ambivalence toward matter and the soul's presence in the body that is observed in Plotinus's earliest treatises (e.g. *Enneads* V.1 and IV.8).[20]   In *Ennead* VI,7.31, Plotinus's overriding concern is the denial that Authentic Beauty ventures into the material sphere. Implicit in this denial is the idea that what does venture into matter (i.e., the soul) is downgraded as a result of this association.

The Gnostic Question

The very issue of Plotinus's possible intellectual evolution is closely aligned with another intriguing one, namely, the nature of his own relationship with the Gnostic tradition. Scholars have long contended that certain aspects of Plotinian philosophy (or the general character of Plotinian thought) exhibits a kinship with Gnosticism.[21] The most notable proponent of this thesis was Hans Jonas, who saw in the *Enneads* a philosophical version of a Gnostic view of reality.[22] In the wake of Jonas's work, other scholars have supported the contention that the *Enneads* exhibit affinities with Gnosticism either on the basis of structural similarities, or on the basis of common imagery and motifs, and various conceptual parallels.[23] In this context, *tolma*-language might be viewed as but another criterion which enables us to assess the possibility of a residual Gnostic element in the *Enneads*.[24]

In the various expressions of the Myth of Sophia that we find preserved in Irenaeus and in the Nag Hammadi writings, *tolma* (or the closely related *authades*) is implicit in the assertiveness and rebellion of a lower principle against a higher one. This willful movement results in a fall into an inferior mode of being, along with its attendant sufferings and evils. The fall transpires either as a punishment for such arrogance, or as a necessary outcome of the separation of the lower principle from its source.

Some interesting parallels are discernible between Plotinus's use of *tolma*-language and the role of *tolma* in certain Nag Hammadi writings. First, Sophia's passionate desire to create on her own (as depicted, for example, in the *Hypostasis of the Archons* 93:34-94:24) exhibits a kinship with Plotinus's description of soul's desire to embark upon an independent course of action (*Enneads* V.1(10).1.1-10), to engage in a direct involvement with bodies, and to venture into the material realm. A second basis of comparison is found in the notion that separation from one's ultimate ground coincides with a forgetfulness of one's origins and, in effect, one's true spiritual identity. This theme is prominent in both *Ennead* V.1(10).1 and in various

Nag Hammadi treatises (e.g. *Treatise Without Title On the Origin of the World* 103:23).

A third parallel is found in the very character of descent that *tolma* prompts: for both Plotinus and some Gnostics, *tolma* coincides with a refusal to participate in the totality of things. In different versions of the Myth of Sophia, Sophia's offspring opts for a separate, autonomous existence (e.g. *Apocryphon of John* 45:13-18; 20-46). The tension that arises as a result of the choice for a partial, circumscribed sphere of influence in lieu of a participation in the totality is likewise evident in Plotinus's discussions of the descent of souls (e.g. *Ennead* IV.8(6).4.10-12; 7.1-14).

As we have seen, such parallel uses of *tolma*-language in Plotinus are not confined to his discussions of the descent of individual souls alone. They are also evident on the level of Nous and the mythical motifs which Plotinus employs in depicting its "standing apart" from the One. Parallels are also found in his discussion of the downward movement of the World Soul (*Ennead* III.7(45).11.15-23) in response to a "restlessly active nature." The spirit of *polupragmon* or an "unquiet power" which Plotinus imputes to the World Soul in this passage exhibits some affinities with *tolma* (albeit in an indirect way).

In light of Plotinus's anti-Gnostic critique, the language of *Ennead* III.7(45).11 strikes me as somewhat surprising. In a very real sense, it is reminiscent of the very fall accounts which Plotinus himself rejected. Perhaps, as I noted above, he only resorted to such a mythical motif in attempting to describe that which transcends the limitations of human consciousness. But the tone of the passage also suggests an uneasiness with Soul's generation of temporal process. In this respect, the exposition displays a kinship with the accounts of *Nous's* descent in *Enneads* VI.9(9).5.24-29, III.8(30).8.31-38, and V.8(31).13.1-11. In these passages, the language conveys a sense of loss and to some extent, even regret over what has transpired. Plotinus seems preoccupied with contrasting what *Nous* and Soul *were* with what they now *are*: their powers dispersed and their faculties weakened, they must relinquish their possession of the whole in favor of a mere groping after images.

But while *tolma* and *polupragmon* do display some similar connotations (as developed in Chapter IV, pp. 114-115 above), they are not exactly the same. By the same token, however, Plotinus could have been reluctant to use *tolma*-language explicitly in the context of a discussion regarding the descent of an aspect of Soul by the time that he formulated the insights surrounding *Ennead* III.7(45).11 (the 45th treatise according to Porphyry's chronological ordering). This reluctance might well have stemmed from the Gnostic flavor of that terminology. Such reservations would be understandable after Plotinus's own sharp criticism (some twelve treatises earlier in *Ennead* II.9) of those who hold that Soul created out of arrogance and audacity.

The hypothesis that *tolma*-language points to a link between Plotinus and the Gnostics must, of course, be carefully approached. Nevertheless, the recognized affinities between Plotinian thought and Gnosticism on various levels raises the possibility that Plotinus's use of *tolma*-language bears a Gnostic influence (or perhaps, that Gnostic uses of *tolma*-language bear a Plotinian influence). I prescind here from offering any firm conclusions on this question, and leave its resolution to those with a more specialized knowledge of Gnosticism and Coptic than I now possess. But I wish to note that the Nag Hammadi library provides some intriguing alternative pictures of Gnosticism that challenge certain mainstream presuppositions. Indeed, much of this material corroborates earlier views of Gnosticism as a movement wholly given over to radically dualistic, anti-cosmic outlooks. But other writings in the Nag Hammadi *corpus* seriously call into question traditional characterizations of Gnostic speculation exclusively in these terms, or else, as no more than simplistic caricatures of Greek philosophy resulting in shallow, fanciful attempts to explain the origin of the world and the human condition.

Cases in point are provided by such Nag Hammadi texts as *Allogenes* and *The Tripartite Tractate*.[25] In *Allogenes* (NHC XI,3), we find a rather sophisticated monistic vision of reality in the context of a discussion that combines revelatory discourse with philosophical elements drawn from the Platonic tradition. *The Tripartite Tractate* (NHC I,5) presents a variation of the Valentinian Myth of Sophia that depicts the generative activity of the Logos (the counterpart of Sophia) in optimistic terms as an ordering of the world.

The Tripartite Tractate is especially interesting in its emphasis upon the emergence of the world on the basis of an emanation of the "Totalities," whereby the Father extends himself toward that which he loves (*The Tripartite Tractate* 73.25,ff.). In this respect, we find an explicit denial that emanation occurs as the result of any severance of the "Totalities" from each other which would likewise estrange them from their source (*The Tripartite Tractate* 73.20,ff.). The Father's extension is accomplished through the intermediary action of the Logos, one of the wise aeons (*The Tripartite Tractate* 75.30-35). Like Sophia, the Logos attempts to understand the unknowableness of the Father. But in contrast to Sophia's bold and tragic movement, the Logos's action (in this case motivated by free will, that is, *autexousios*) is directed toward a fundamentally good end, namely, to give glory to the Father by communicating his love (*The Tripartite Tractate* 76.4). While the world which issues from this action is depicted as imperfect and defective, the reader is cautioned against criticizing the Logos's movement. In effect, it is viewed as the cause of an order which has been ordained to emerge (*The Tripartite Tractate* 77.5-10). Here, we find an attempt to reconcile the Logos's downward tendency or fall with the demands of a higher law that is somewhat reminiscent of what we find in Plotinus's later psychological deliberations.

Apparently, *The Tripartite Tractate* does not employ *tolma*-language in its discussion of the Logos's descent. However, its attribution of this downward movement to *autexousios* calls to mind the voluntarism and spirit of venturesomeness inherent in Plotinian *tolma*. But while parallels between Plotinus and the Gnostics regarding the use of *tolma* (or related language) can be established, important differences are evident as well. To begin with, *tolma* is never responsible for a real rupture or faultline in Plotinus's scheme, as it is in the more radically dualistic Gnostic systems. That sort of upheaval is suggested in *Zostrianos* (128:10-14), which imputes the lower aeons' confinement to matter (and by implication, the generation of the material world) to *tolma* (along with the knowledge of greatness and power). Plotinus may have been referring to this very account (among others) in his indictment of the Gnostic claim that the world was generated out of *tolma*. Moreover, even the optimism of *The Tripartite Tractate* (with its strong suggestion of the operation of *tolma*) is tinged with pessimism regarding the long-range effects of the Logos's descent: his descent results, we are informed, in a division (77.20-25) which precipitates "sicknesses" and upheavals (79-80.10).

Another important divergence is recognized by Atkinson, who contends that Sophia's *tolma* (as depicted in Valentinian schemes) prompts "an upward rather than a downward movement."[26]   In this sense, the Valentinians viewed *tolma* as the origin of an attempt to usurp the Father's power. But in this context, Atkinson not only contrasts Gnostic and Plotinian *tolma*, but Gnostic and Neopythagorean usages of the term as well.[27] (The Neopythagoreans, as we have seen, explicitly connected *tolma* with the Dyad and the downward procession of being.)   Atkinson's point brings to the fore a potential argument against the attempt to read a Gnostic element into Plotinian *tolma*. From this standpoint, Plotinus's use of *tolma*-language might be regarded as consistent with later Pythagoreanism rather than with Gnosticism. This may well be the case, at least in regard to *tolma's* appearance in Plotinus's account of the descent of *Nous*. But such a clear-cut distinction between the metaphysical schema of the Pythagoreans and Gnostics is not altogether valid.

It must be borne in mind that our knowledge of this period and its intellectual developments is still highly fragmentary. Later Platonists and Pythagoreans might have shared more in common with the Gnostics than is generally acknowledged. In this respect, the possibility of reciprocal influences between Neopythagoreanism, certain expressions of Gnosticism, and Neoplatonism cannot be ruled out completely.[28] Through the efforts of scholars like Jonas, Elsas, and De Vogel, Plotinus can be viewed as a participant in a milieu that included a wide variety of philosophical and theological sources.[29]   From this standpoint, it would be erroneous to view him as completely distinct from the other intellectual currents of his time. This is a relevant consideration when assessing the sources and background of *tolma*-language in Plotinus. Such a consideration directs us back to the issue addressed at the outset of this chapter concerning Plotinus's intellectual evolution.

Does the fact that Plotinus no longer used *tolma*-language (except in *Ennead* VI.7(38).31) after his anti-Gnostic polemic mean (as Dodds implied) that Plotinus divorced himself from an prior allegiance to Gnosticism? Despite Plotinus's own statement that he numbered certain Gnostics among his "friends" (*Ennead* II.9(33).10), no evidence exists that he could have ever been classified as a "Gnostic."[30] But his apparent reluctance to use *tolma*-language after his reaction against the Gnostics still suggests a desire on his part to transform an earlier pessimism toward the emergence of being into an more optimistic outlook.

In the final analysis, however, the real issue is not whether Plotinus rejected *tolma*-language at a certain juncture in his intellectual career. The real issue, I think, is whether the tension between optimistic and pessimistic attitudes toward otherness, differentiation, and plurality extends into Plotinus's "mature" writings, that is, those writings subsequent to the anti-Gnostic polemic. In this respect, the actual use of *tolma*-language becomes irrelevant. What is most relevant is what the later Plotinus has to say about reality other than the One.

Plotinus's Residual Pessimism

While the overwhelming number of Plotinus's writings praise the beauty, harmony, and diversity of the lower orders of reality, there remain those nagging passages which either lament the emergence of otherness or which suggest that unity is preferable to multiplicity.[31] In some places, Plotinus questions whether it was even necessary for anything other than the One to exist. This uneasiness with plurality is evident at all stages of Plotinus's intellectual development.

The early *Ennead* I.6 (first treatise in Porphyry's chronology) displays a marked devaluation of matter and the world of sense experience. In Plotinian terms, the lower world represents the antithesis of that genuine Beauty which is found only in the intelligible world. But the same sentiments are evident in the rather late *Ennead* I.8 (fifty-first treatise in chronological order), which designates matter as the basis of evil, a principle almost completely devoid of the One's goodness and power. Yet, Plotinus's most glaring indictment of plurality is found in *Ennead* III.8.8. 35-36 (the first treatise in his anti-Gnostic polemic and thirtieth in chronological order), a passage which suggests an uneasiness with *Nous's* very emergence as a distinct hypostasis: ". . . how better for it not to desire this, for it became second!"

Now, it might be argued that this constitutes but an isolated utterance that fails to reflect Plotinus's fully developed viewpoint.[32] But one finds a number of other passages scattered throughout the *Enneads* that bespeak a pessimism toward the very fact of otherness. In a rational scheme based upon the rational deduction of all things from the One, plurality must imply a deficiency of goodness, life, and power; anything other than the One must be less than the One. If perfection lies in pure unity, however, why should anything other than the One exist?[33] Similar sentiments are found in the later *Ennead* VI.4(22).1, which likewise characterizes plurality in terms of a deficiency.[34] There, Plotinus suggests that multiplicity reflects a failure to remain whole and self-contained. In this respect, it is assumed that what is unified is superior to that which is multiple and diversified.[35]

Interestingly, these sentiments emerge (on the basis of the chronological ordering of writings) either after or around the same time as Plotinus's anti-Gnostic polemic. Yet, even at this later stage of his intellectual development, he still exhibits that ambivalence toward the manifold that we encounter in the early writings: on the one hand, plurality must be good, because it proceeds from the One; on the other hand, plurality is characterized as fallen, deficient, and even evil because it is the result of a voluntary descent from the One's absolute unity and perfection.

Conclusion

In one sense, Plotinus's use of *tolma*-language (and his reliance upon the various fall-accounts in which it appears) can be explained on the basis of the exigencies of his metaphysics. But in this regard, we encounter a built-in tension in Plotinian thought, precisely because Plotinus the rationalist resorted to a non-rational account in coming to terms with the fact of otherness. The *Enneads* reflect a struggle on his part between an intellectual commitment to a positive conception of being and the dictates of a temperment which viewed plurality and diversity in disparaging terms.

Plotinus made an attempt to reconcile these two positions. This is especially evident in his later claim that the descent of individual souls is consistent with the prescriptions of law. The end result was a rather uneasy theory which depicted souls as both fallen and "sent" to order and govern bodies. But the very fact that Plotinus attempted such a synthesis suggests a certain discomfort with the presence of souls in a material environment. To a great extent, he was struggling with a problem that he had inherited from Plato. But the problem was also very much his own. A pessimism toward otherness is evident in those passages which utilize *tolma* (or closely related language). But even when such terminology does not appear (i.e. in Plotinus's later writings), one can find a number of texts which convey a sense of pessimism toward the manifold.

Notes

1. Hans Jonas, "The Soul in Gnosticism and Plotinus," in *Le Néoplatonisme* (Royaumant, 1971), p. 53. Jonas's remarks are directed toward a characterization of Soul, but they are applicable to Plotinus's use of *tolma*-language in general.

2. *Ennead* III.8(30).1.13-18.

3. *Ennead* V.8(31).7.17-25. In this context, matter is treated in rather positive terms, an approach which contrasts sharply with that of the later *Ennead* I.8(51).

4. *Ennead* V.8(31).1.38-40.

5. *Ennead* III.8(30).3.12-17; V.8(31).4.35-39.

6. *Ennead* V.5(32).1.38-41.

7. *Ennead* II.9(33).1.12-19.

8. *Ennead* II.9(33).2.6-10.

9. *Ennead* II.9(33).4.1-4.

10. *Ennead* II.9(33).7.1-7.

11. *Ennead* II.9(33).8.1-5.

12. This myth, as recounted by Irenaeus, was especially prominent among the Valentinian Gnostics.

13. *Ennead* II.9(33).10.17-18. At this point in the discussion (lines 3-5), Plotinus adds a personal note, referring to those gnostics whom he numbered among his "friends."

14. *Ennead* II.9(33).11.19-22.

15. E. R. Dodds, *Pagan and Christian In An Age of Anxiety* (Cambridge: Cambridge University Press, 1968), 25-26. Dodds asserts that Plotinus's earlier work reflects the more pessimistic attitude toward the soul favored by the Pythagoreans and the Gnostics (citing *Enneads* IV.7, V.1, and IV.8). He cites three passages (*Enneads* VI.9.5, V.1.1, and V.2.2) where Plotinus uses *tolma*-language to designate the soul's deliberate

choice for descent. Dodds cites *Enneads* IV.3.13 and IV.4.11 as texts which are representative of Plotinus's "mature" viewpoint: in these places, descent is linked with the dictates of cosmic law.

16. H.R. Schwyzer, "Plotinus," *Real-Encycklopaedie der Klassischen Altertum- wissenschaft, Pauly-Wissowa-Kroll-*Witter (Stuttgard, 1894, ff.), XXI, 1, cols. 547-548. cf. more recent studies by H. Ch. Puech, "Plotin et les Gnos- tiques" in *Les Sources de Plotin* (Vandoeuvres-Geneve, 1960): 161-190; C. Elsas, *Neuplatonische und gnostische Weltablehnung in der Schule Plotins* (Berlin, 1975).

17. A.H. Armstrong, translation of Plotinus's *Enneads*, Loeb Classical Library, Volume II (Cambridge, Mass.: Harvard University Press; Lon- don: William Heinemann, Ltd., 1966), p. 226, n. 1. The vehemence of Plotinus's reaction against the Gnostics (coupled with pessimistic senti- ments toward reality other than the One) have prompted some to find a special significance in the "long treatise"—that is, *Enneads* III.8(30), V.8(31), V.5(32), and II,9(33). In this regard, Katz ("Plotinus and the Gnostics," *Journal of the History of Ideas* XV (1954): 289) made the follow- ing observations, almost forty years ago: ". . . it is amazing that almost all of the ideas that Plotinus finds objectionable in the Gnostics have been asserted by himself too in one form or another. The polemic against the Gnostics . . . turns out to reveal a vital tension in Plotinus's own system, rather than a mere external differentiation of his doctrines from others. To see Plotinus as in some sense a Gnostic *manqué* is to discover an important aspect of his many-faceted philosophy. In the essay against the Gnostics Plotinus, who usually is very restrained, permits himself a large amount of emotional invective. This too suggests that we are touching upon a vital nerve of Plotinus's thought. While Katz's characterization of Plotinus as "in some sense a Gnostic *manqué*" is excessive, his perception of a tension in Plotinus's scheme (vis à vis the anti-Gnostic treatises) is rather thought-provoking. In a similar vein, Sinnige (in Plotinus *Amid Gnostics And Christians*, edited by David T. Runia (Amsterdam: Free University Press, 1984), p. 77) has more recently suggested that the so- called "long treatise" represents something of a "crisis point" in Ploti- nus's outlook which injects new life into the question of a possible devel- opment in his philosophical theories.

18. Rist articulates this view in a review of Dodd's *Pagan And Christian In An Age of Anxiety* in Phoenix 20 (1966): 350.

19. J. M. Rist, *Plotinus: The Road To Reality*, p. 257, n. 3: "It is true that at 3.7.11.15ff. Plotinus ascribes to the World Soul the desire to rule itself and to be its own master (ἄρχειν αὐτῆς βουλομένη καὶ εἶναι αὐτῆς) and that this is comparable to the τὸ βουληθῆναι δὲ ἑαυτῶν εἶναι of individual souls in 5.1.1, but the context of the two passages is different. In 5.1.1 Plotinus is speaking of the origin of sin—which for individual

souls co-exists with free-will; in 3.7.11 (where the word *tolma* does not occur) he is dealing with the purely cosmological activity of the World Soul to which no sinfulness need be attached per se."

20. *Ennead* VI.7(38).31: μὴ γὰρ ἂν τολμῆσαι ἐκεῖνα οἷά ἐστιν εἰς βόρβορον σωμάτων ἐμβῆναι καὶ ῥυπᾶναι ἑαυτὰ καὶ ἀφανίσαι.

21. Th. G. Sinnige offers a concise overview of these scholarly trends in "Gnostic Influences in the early works of Plotinus and in Augustine," in *Plotinus Amid Gnostics and Christians*, pp. 73-97.

22. e.g. *Gnosis und spätantiker Geist*, volumes I, II (Gottingen, 1934-1954); *The Gnostic Religion*, 2nd edition (Boston: Beacon Press, 1963); "The Soul in Gnosticism and Plotinus," *Néoplatonisme* (Royaumant, 1971), pp. 45-53.

23. Major sources which should be included in this group are: H. Ch. Puech, "Plotin it les Gnostiques"; J. Zandee, *The terminology of Plotinus and of some Gnostic writings, Mainly the Fourth Treatise of the Jung Codex* (Istanbul, 1961); C. Elsas, *Neuplatonische und gnostische Weltablehnung in der Schule Plotins*.

24. cf. J. Zandee, *The terminology of Plotinus and of some Gnostic writings . . .*, pp. 26-28.

25. Porphyry, it will be remembered, referred to "revelations by Zoroaster and Zostrianos and Nicotheus and Allogenes and Messus and other people of this kind" that had been composed by "sectarians who had abandoned the old philosophy" (αἱρετικοὶ δὲ ἐκ τῆς παλαιᾶς φιλοσοφίας ἀνηγμένοι) and which were attacked by Plotinus (*Vita Plotini* 16). Whether the "Allogenes" to whom Porphyry alludes was the author of the Nag Hammadi writing which bears that title is debatable. The monistic and triadic emphasis that we find in that work, however, clearly distinguishes it from radically dualistic expressions of Gnosticism. The same is true of *The Tripartite Tractate*. For a discussion of Porphyry's reference, see J. Igal, "The Gnostics and 'The Ancient Philosophy' in Porphyry and Plotinus," ·in *Neoplatonism and Early Christian Thought. Essays in Honour of A.H. Armstrong*. Edited by H.J. Blumenthal and R.A. Markus (London: Variorum Publishers, Ltd., 1981), pp. 138-149.

26. Michael Atkinson, *Plotinus: Ennead V.1 On the Three Principal Hypostases. A Commentary with Translation* (Oxford: Oxford University Press, 1983). Commentary on *Ennead* V.1.4 (p. 5)

27. Ibid., pp. 4-5.

28. For a discussion of these links, see the discussion following Ch. Puech's essay "Plotin et les Gnostiques" (especially the exchange between Dodds, Puech, and Henry, pp. 178-180).

29. For the contributions of Jonas and Elsas, see notes #22 and 23, above. For the contributions of C.J. DeVogel, see "On the Neoplatonic Character of Platonism and the Platonic Character of Neoplatonism," *Mind* 62 (1953): 43-64; and *Greek Philosophy. A Collection of Texts with Notes and Translations*, volume III (Leiden: E.J. Brill, 1959), pp. 408, ff.

30. *Ennead* II.9 (33) .10.3-5: Αἰδὼς γάρ τις ἡμᾶς ἔχει πρός τινας τῶν φίλων, οἳ τούτῳ τῷ λόγῳ ἐντυχόντες πρότερον ἢ ἡμῖν φίλοι γενέσθαι οὐκ οἶδ' ὅπως ἐπ' αὐτοῦ μένουσι.

    Dodds' assertion (see note #15, above) that a change came when Plotinus "breaks finally with Gnosticism" can be rather misleading. At first glance, it might be taken to mean that Plotinus himself was once a Gnostic, and then, severed that earlier association. While there is no real evidence to substantiate such a thesis (other than some apparent affinities between Plotinus and Gnosticism), scholars do support the view that the early Plotinus was amenable to a pessimism consistent with Gnostic, Hermetic and Neopythagorean dualism.

31. Plotinus's treatises "On Providence" (*Enneads* III.2(47). and III.3(48), are especially rich in praise for the cosmos.

32. A.H. Armstrong, "*Gnosis and Greek Philosophy*" (p. 118), suggests that ". . . the passage represents a passing emotional intensification of the mystic's sense of the worthlessness of all things in comparison with the Absolute Good . . ."

33. *Ennead* V.1(10).6.1-8.

34. *Ennead* VI.5(23).12.19-22: ἀλλ' ὅτι καὶ ἄλλο τι προσῆν σοι μετὰ τὸ 'πᾶς', ἐλάττων ἐγίνου τῇ προσθήκῃ· οὐ γὰρ ἐκ τοῦ ὄντος ἦν ἡ προσθήκη . . . ἀλλὰ τοῦ μὴ ὄντος.

    cf. *Ennead* VI.6(34).1.4-6: καὶ γὰρ πολὺ ἕκαστον, ὅταν ἀδυνατοῦν εἰς αὐτὸ νεύειν χέηται καὶ ἐκείνηται σκιδνάμενον· καὶ πάντη μὲν στερικόμενον ἐν τῇ χύσει τοῦ ἑνὸς πλῆθος γίνεσθαι, οὐκ ὄντος τοῦ ἄλλο πρὸς ἄλλο μέρος αὐτοῦ ἐνοῦντος.

35. *Ennead* VI.7(38).8.22.

Epilogue

"Each of us," wrote Thomas Wolfe, "is all the sums he has not counted . . ."[1] Wolfe's observation, it seems, assumes a special relevance in regard to the consideration of a philosophical point of view such as we find in Plotinus. For, the elements that contribute to the development of a thinker are many and varied. One cannot, for example, overlook the crucial role played by personal experience. Such experience encompasses one's entire background, including the many relationships, intellectual and non-intellectual interests, and decisive episodes that punctuate any life-history. In the final analysis, the philosophical stance which one adopts says something vital not only about one's goals as a thinker, but about the influences which shape one as a thinker as well. An effective means of delineating these influences was provided by the intellectual historian W.C.K. Guthrie, who maintained that philosophies are the products of three distinct but complementary factors: the temperament of the individual philosopher, the external environment which philosophers inhabit, and the influence of previous philosophers upon a given thinker. [2]

Let us first examine the issue regarding "external environment," that is, the world as it presents itself to a thinker. This issue, in turn, touches upon the question regarding the historical dimension of philosophical outlooks. In my opinion, the philosophical enterprise represents an ongoing attempt to encounter the world from various perspectives, to analyze critically and clarify the fundamental questions and problems which challenge us as human beings, and to search for the most suitable explanation. From this standpoint, philosophy is very much a human activity that reflects all of the complexity of human existence. But contrary to popular belief, philosophers do not dwell upon some rarefied stratum. Rather, they are living personages who respond to the issues and crises of their own time, and whose philosophizing frequently reflects the spirit of their own age.

Plotinus was the product of a Hellenistic environment that exposed him to a wide range of social, political, and cultural influences. Among these, we must include his Alexandrian background, his exposure to a wide range of philosophical and religious approaches, his widespread travels (perhaps as far as India), his familiarity with classical Greek sources, and his acquaintance with Gnosticism (and through some exponents of this tradition, quite possibly with Christianity as well).

To a great extent, Plotinus was a man of his age. The third century, A.D. (the period which Dodds characterized as the "age of anxiety") was a time of uncertainty and insecurity on all levels.[3] Confronted with widespread political, social, and moral upheaval, people were prompted to question their fundamental beliefs and to speculate about the meaning of human existence. Philosophy now merged with religion, expressing the deepest cravings within human nature. This introspective spirit permeated society as a whole, and even penetrated imperial circles: in the words of Marcus Aurelius, the philosopher-emperor, philosophy became a "kind of priest and minister of the gods."[4] Plotinian thought, with its emphasis upon the possibility of individual salvation, could readily find a receptive audience in such a starved intellectual and spiritual environment.

Frequently, philosophizing involves a response to (or reaction against) the ideas of one's predecessors. In this context, we might (taking Guthrie's lead) include reflection upon previous thinkers in a tentative list of historical influences which shape a philosophical viewpoint. The question might be framed in this manner: to what extent do previous philosophies inspire, define, and limit a thinker's position?

Plotinus's preoccupation with the relationship between unity and plurality, his struggle over the question regarding souls' involvement with Nature and bodily existence, and his concern with the problem of evil reflect his participation in the classical Greek philosophical tradition. First and foremost, Plotonius's thought was rooted in Platonism. To a lesser degree, it exhibits an adaptation of Aristotelian and Stoic elements. But Plotinus's deliberations cannot be approached against the background of classical sources alone. An adequate assessment of the *Enneads* must address Plotinus's response to developments in later Greek philosophy. In this respect, Plotinus's thinking bore the imprint of insights current in Middle Platonism and later Pythagoreanism. But it also displays an occasional commonground with some of the eclectic religious movements (e.g. Hermeticism and Gnosticism) of the Hellenistic age. This is especially evident in Plotinus's pessimistic accounts of the descent of being which rely upon the use of *tolma* (or related language) in discussing the motive for the emergence of reality other than the One.

But the ideas of any significant thinker are not confined to a single historical period. The mark of a great mind is the ability to transcend a given time and the capacity to speak to people of future times with force and clarity. In this sense, a focus upon the historical dimension of intellectual activity alone might imply that philosophizing is wholly dependent upon historical processes, that philosophies are no more than "stimulus responses" to one's external environment, and that philosophical thinking is restricted exclusively to a particular spatio-temporal setting. If one is to avoid a purely historicist interpretation, other explanatory factors must be proposed.

We come to what is possibly the most significant factor addressed by Guthrie, namely, the temperament of a philosopher and its impact upon his or her outlook. This factor brings to the fore the psychological dimension of philosophical activity and those influences which might be characterized in terms of what William James called the "passional nature"—that side of human belief which is shaped by feeling, personal preferences, and uncritical assumptions rather than by insight, logic, and dispassionate reason alone.[5] But how are we to interpret "temperament" (or, in Jamesian parlance, the "passional nature") and how can we measure its influence upon a thinker? Such questions, of course, can never be answered in any definitive way. Indeed, we must approach them with great caution, lest we slip into the nebulous (and highly questionable) realm of "psycho-history." But given the complexity of human thought, one must at least acknowledge the operation of a variety of emotions and affectivities upon our cognitive life.

From a philosophical standpoint, such influences might well determine the very problems that a thinker deems worthy of consideration, or the way in which they are treated.

To what extent did Plotinus's temperament or passional instincts influence the development of his philosophy? As I have just observed, such a question only admits of highly speculative conclusions. However, on the basis of the evidence provided by the *Enneads*, it appears that Plotinus's early attachment to pessimistic sentiments persisted long after he had rejected them on rational grounds. Plotinus was deeply rooted in the rationalist tradition. But one perceives that he felt estranged from the material world until the end of his life. Although the *Enneads* are filled with imagery that is highly sensual and grounded in nature, the reader continually confronts a sense of alienation from the visible world which finds expression in Plotinus's otherworldly orientation.

As we have seen, the *Enneads* exhibit a tension between an optimistic emanation/diffusion account and a series of pessimistic accounts. On the one side, Plotinus was committed to the entire thrust of Hellenistic rationalism; on the other side, he relied upon fall motifs in explaining the emergence of reality. This latter side of Plotinian thought reveals itself in the view that unity is preferable to multiplicity and that, perhaps, the manifold should have never emerged.

Scholars have tended to minimize the importance of such statements, or to mitigate their force by balancing them against the greater number of passages which praise the beauty and harmony of the world. However, it is precisely such pessimistic statements which merit closer attention. For the true temperament of a thinker might well reveal itself in just those assertions which seem anomolous or inconsistent with the general character of his or her outlook. In Plotinus, we find a thinker who was deeply committed to Hellenic rationalism and the positive conception of being and the cosmos which grew out of that tradition. But the *Enneads* reflect a tension between this positive outlook and the dictates of an otherworldly temperament which sought to transcend a changing and unreliable world of sense experience. The evidence before us suggests that Plotinian thought took shape not only on the basis of intellectual considerations, but non-intellectual, non-rational ones as well.

Notes

1. Thomas Wolfe, *Look Homeward, Angel* (New York: Charles Scribner's Sons, 1929, 1957), p. 3.

2. W. C. K. Guthrie, *The Greek Philosophers From Thales To Aristotle* (New York: Harper Colophon, 1975), p. 19. The philosopher Karl Jaspers also provides some interesting remarks regarding the historical dimension of philosophizing in his *Way to Wisdom* (New Haven: Yale University Press, 1962, p. 135): "We understand the historical manifestations of the truth only if we examine it in conjunction with the world in which it arose and the destinies of the men who conceived it. The history of philosophy comes alive for us when, by thorough study of a work and of the world in which it was produced, we participate as it were in that work. After that we seek perspectives which will afford us a view of the history of philosophy as a whole . . ."

3. E. R. Dodds, *Pagan And Christian In An Age Of Anxiety* (Cambridge: Cambridge University Press, 1968), p. 3. Dodd's study of the emergence of Christianity and its reception by the non-Christian world takes the third century, A.D. as its point of departure. Dodds' characterizes this period as a time of "barbarian invasions, bloody civil wars, recurrent epidemics, galloping inflation, and extreme . . . insecurity."

4. Samuel Dill, *Roman Society From Nero to Marcus Aurelius* (London: Macmillan, 1920), p. 248.

5. William James, "The Will to Believe," in *Classical and Contemporary Readings in the Philosophy of Religion*, second edition, edited by John Hick (Englewood Cliffs, New Jersey: Prentice-Hall, 1970), pp. 219-220: ". . . our intellectual nature does influence our convictions . . . and pure insight and logic . . . are not the only things that really do produce our creeds."

Appendix A

The Ascent to the One in Plotinus

The primary focus of the foregoing study has been Plotinus's metaphysical account of the descending movement of being from the One. But at least some attention must be directed to another major aspect of Plotinus's thought, namely, his account of the ascending movement of all things to their source which complements the descent of being. While Plotinus presents a highly refined rational interpretation of the intelligible and material orders, the *Enneads* also contain a pronounced *religio-mystical* character that is inextricably bound up with key metaphysical themes. We have in this last great thinker of the ancient world what Dean Inge called a "profoundly religious philosophy" and what Philip Merlan characterized as a "mysticism of reason," or more precisely, a "rationalistic mysticism."[1] An examination of the mystical element in Plotinian thought directs us to the *epistrophe* that parallels emanation and descent at all levels.

Any consideration of Plotinus's mystical element must begin with the One, since this supreme first principle constitutes both the source of all things and the end toward which everything aspires.[2] While the One is a transcendent source of power and life, it is nonetheless accessible to those individuals capable of sufficiently detaching themselves from "otherness" and the life of the senses.[3] But it is the individual who must seek after the One; the One seeks no union with individuals. Moreover (as *Ennead* VI.4(22).11.1-10 affirms), participation is contingent upon the fitness of the participant.

Plotinus rules out any possibility of pantheism, emphasizing the absolute aloofness of the One.[4] Despite this aloofness, the One is immanent within the whole of reality, in the manner suggested by Plotinus's solar radiation metaphors. In this regard, Plotinian mysticism also has been characterized as a "theistic" mysticism: rather than stressing a realization of self as identical with the One, Plotinus stresses the conformity of self with the One's simplicity, a state attainable by means of contemplation, moral purification, and the renunciation of material attachments.[5] Plotinus always upholds the "ontological difference" between the absolutely transcendent One and its effects.

The relationship of dependence between the One and its effects provides the very foundation of Plotinian mysticism. In this regard, the Platonic appellation of the "Good" is most appropriate for the One, since this principle constitutes the ultimate object of desire, the final end toward which everything tends. The Platonic identification of the One with the Good (which assumes great significance in Plotinian thought) was subsequently transmitted into the Christian mystical tradition. [6]

The first step in the attainment of "*unio-mystica,*" (that is, mystical union with the One), is the ascent of the soul to the level of *Nous*. In *Ennead* V.3(49), the treatise on "*The Knowing Hypostases,*" Plotinus maintains that a bond exists between each of us as thinking subjects and *Nous*. True self-knowledge is characterized as the state in which the knower and that which is known are the same: the knowing subject must be identified with the object of intellection.[7] The object which is known is identical with *Nous*, the principle containing all reality within itself. Since *Nous* and the intellectual object are living, existent realities, they are identified as one. Self-knowledge, therefore, is the result of a harmonization of the act of intellection and the intellectual object with *Nous*.

The act of knowing admits of no separation between subject and object. Rather, these principles coalesce under the guidance of *Nous*. By means of its identification with *Nous*, the intellect of the individual being is transformed and elevated to a higher intellectual plane, taking with it the soul's higher part.[8] Individual intellects achieve such self-transcendence when they free themselves of all extraneous concerns and engage in contemplative activity.[9]

The soul's ascent to the life of *Nous*, with its accompanying demand for moral purification and a withdrawal from worldly concerns, provides the basis of Plotinian mysticism on its most personal level, that is, the return of the individual soul to the One. For Plotinus, mystical knowledge satisfies the human yearning for unity, a yearning which Emile Brehier described as "the fundamental aspiration of reason." [10]

Plotinus affirms that this quest for unity is an instinctive human tendency. Unification is achieved by means of interiorization, a turning within oneself to find one's true spiritual identity. While the One is absolutely transcendent, souls remain close to it. They are never completely excised from their source regardless of their degree of immersion in worldly pursuits. In order to attain this heightened level of spirituality, souls must undergo a process of moral purification through the life of virtue. Contemplation also provides the soul with the proper disposition to renounce material attachments. [11]

Love plays a crucial role in the soul's ascent to the One. The image of the union of lovers expresses the soul's yearning for unification with its ontological ground. In metaphysical terms, love provides a kind of dynamic, driving force which motivates the soul upward.[12] Brehier links Plotinus's discussion of love in this context with the Platonic notion of *eros*, the universal urge which directs all things toward the ultimate Good.[13] Souls already possess something of the divine, and once perceiving this kinship, they are filled with a passionate desire for union with their source, like lovers who long for union with the beloved.[14]

The drive for union spurred on by love culminates in the soul's ascent to the One. Love renders possible the similitude which is the goal of mystical experience. Through love, Plotinus maintains, we become god-like. In his powerful accounts of mystical experience, the soul's vision of the One occurs instantaneously, like a "leap" which is both tranquil and effortless: we must not force the experience or "chase after it," Plotinus cautions, "but wait quietly till it appears."[15] This "leap" culminates in an illumination by the One and a unification with the divine through consciousness.

The foregoing sketch of Plotinus's mysticism affords us but a brief glimpse of an extremely profound aspect of his thought. Plotinus's originality as a thinker is evident in the manner in which his treatment of the soul's ascent is skillfully interwoven into the fabric of his metaphysics.[16] While the soul's return to the One can be approached purely in terms of religious experience, it also constitutes a component of cosmic process. The soul's yearning for unification (inspired by *eros*), provides the catalyst whereby being returns to the primal unity from which it advanced. The impulse of *eros* implicit in the soul's return to the One counterbalances the "will to otherness" which proceeds from the One's self-diffusiveness. The fusion of the disparate elements of reality through the integrative action of love complements the radical drive toward differentiation, fragmentation, and dispersion. This "will to otherness," as we have observed, manifests itself as *tolma*, the urge for separate existence and autonomy which accounts for the emergence of any plurality in the Plotinian scheme.

Notes

1. W. R. Inge, *Mysticism in Religion* (London: Rider and Co., 1969), p. 158; Philip Merlan, *Monopsychism, Mysticism, Metaconsciousness* (The Hague: Martinus Nijhoff, 1963), p. 2.

2. In his paper, "The Parmenides of Plato and the Origins of Neoplatonic One" (*Classical Quarterly* 22(1928): 140-141), E. R. Dodds refers to the suggestion of J. Geffcken that Plotinus's personal experience of "*unio-mystica*" determined his conception of the One. Dodds contends that "it is perhaps truer to say that his conception of the One determined . . . not . . . the personal experience . . . but the interpretation which Plotinus attached to that experience."

3. *Ennead* VI.9(9).8.33-41.

4. *Ennead* V.5(32).12.40-49.

5. Plotinian mysticism has been characterized as "theistic" by various notable scholars, including John Rist (*Plotinus: The Road to Reality*, p. 228) and A. H. Armstrong (*The Cambridge History of Later Greek and Early Medieval Philosophy*, Cambridge, 1970, p. 263). The latter describes theistic mysticism as ". . . an approach in which the soul seeks to attain a union with the Absolute of which the best earthly analogy is the union of lovers, not a mysticism in which the soul seeks to realize itself as Absolute . . ."

    The characterization of Plotinian mysticism as "theistic" is derived from R. C. Zaehner's statement on mystical experience, *Mysticism Sacred and Profane* (Oxford, 1980, p. 180), which describes "theistic" mystics in this way: ". . . according to them the end of man is not to participate in God in the mode of an 'insensible object' . . . but in the mode that is specific to the mystic as human person, as an individual substance of rational nature, and as the image of God Himself."

6. Dean Inge, *Mysticism in Religion*, p. 205.

7. *Enneads* V.3(49).4.4-14; 5.44-48.

8. *Enneads* V.3(49).4.14-27.

9. *Ennead* V.3(49).4.28-30.

10. Emile Brehier, *The Philosophy of Plotinus*, trans. Joseph Thomas (Chicago, 1971), p. 162.

11. *Enneads* VI.9(9).7.16-23; I.2(19).3.11-22.

12. *Enneads* VI.7(38).34.14-16; III.5(50).4.6-18.

13. Emile Brehier, *The Philosophy of Plotinus*, p. 149.

14. *Enneads* VI.7(38).22.1-11; 31.11-18.

15. *Ennead* V.5(32).8.3-5.

16. Paul Henry, "The Place of Plotinus in the History of Thought," Introduction to Stephen MacKenna's translation of the *Enneads* (New York: Pantheon Books, 1969), pp. lxiv-lxx.

Appendix B

Plotinian *Tolma* and St. Augustine's Treatment of *Superbia*[1]

In concluding this study, I wish to address a final question: what were the long-range effects of Plotinus's account of the descent of being? This question assumes some importance when we consider Plotinus's impact upon the history of medieval Christian thought and especially, upon the intellectual development of St. Augustine of Hippo. While any in-depth analysis of the topic is beyond the scope of this study, it is at least worth a brief consideration. In recent years, the question of Augustine's intellectual relationship to Neoplatonism has received great attention.[2] The various works by Robert J. O'Connell, S.J. (and others) have ably demonstrated the degree to which Augustine might have relied upon the *Enneads* as a philosophical base and the process whereby he creatively adapted and recast Plotinian insights in the interests of his own Christian philosophy. [3]

In the present context, I wish to examine some conceptual links between Plotinian *tolma* and *superbia*, the "beginning of all sin" in Augustine's early account of the fall of the soul. The kinship between Plotinian *tolma* and St. Augustine's moral triad of pride (*superbia*), curiosity (*curiositas*), and carnal concupiscence (*concupiscentia carnis*) has been addressed by various scholars, from different perspectives.[4] In what follows, I will survey the evidence supporting the view that Plotinian *tolma* provides a key to understanding the problematic motive for the soul's movement from God. I will test the hypothesis of a Plotinian "pattern" in the early Augustine, highlighting *tolma's* effectiveness as a tool for unravelling the complexities of Augustine's moral triad, with a specific focus upon its affinities with *superbia*, the root of that triad.

Superbia: Root of the Triad

Augustine isolated pride, that is, *superbia* (or one of its variants—ambition (*ambitio*), the desire for popular renown (*gloria popularis*), or the desire for vain glory) as the chief sin or the gravest of sins.[5] As defined by Augustine, *superbia* constitutes a willful exaltation of self which prompts the soul to abandon its proper mid-rank position between God and lesser creatures.[6] Through the agency of *superbia*, the soul rejects its subordinate role in relation to God, its *Summum Bonum*. *Superbia* initiates a "standing-apart-from-God" (*apostatare a Deo*): the proud soul aspires to an autonomous existence, living for itself (*ad seipsam*) and through itself (*per seipsam*).[7] In the words of the *De libero arbitrio* (II,19,53), the proud soul turns to a good proper to itself alone (*ad proprium*), desiring self-mastery and self-determination. But *superbia* introduces an additional difficulty: the proud soul directs itself to inferior levels of reality, choosing lesser goods as objects of desire, devotion, and love. It exalts those things which it should rightfully govern and use as a means of attaining spiritual perfection and lasting happiness. The proud soul thereby violates the "rule of perfect religion" articulated in the *De Vera Religione*: to serve the Creator rather than the creature and resist vanity in one's thoughts.[8]

By shifting the soul's focus from God to oneself, *superbia* opens the individual to the pull of curiosity (the lust for experiential knowledge through the mediation of the bodily senses) and to the influence of carnal concupiscence (the lust for the gratification of the flesh). If the soul had not succumbed to *superbia*, it might never experience the lust of the eyes and of the flesh. In this respect, *superbia* assumes a "root character" as the beginning of all sin (cf. *Ecclesiasticus* 10:9-14) and the prime motive for the soul's aversion from God.

Superbia and Tolma: Primal Faults

In several passages, Augustine cites the Scriptural text of *Ecclesiasticus* (10:9-14) as support for the contention that *superbia* is the beginning of sin.[9] One finds an excellent Plotinian counterpart for *superbia* in *tolma*, the term which Plotinus used to designate the prime motive for the soul's fall into material bodies and its direct involvement in temporal process. In what sense is this so? In order to answer this question, we must first turn to the *locus classicus* of *tolma*-language in the *Enneads*, that is, *Ennead* V.1(10).1.1-10, and its explicit designation of *tolma* as the origin of evil for the soul. In this context, *tolma* constitutes a willful desire for otherness, differentiation, temporal process, and self-determination.

In contrast to Plotinian emanationism, Augustine proceeded from the Judeo-Christian tenet of creation *ex nihilo* by a personal, providential God. While the Plotinian One is determined by its own nature to emanate and generate being, the Judeo-Christian God engages in a free creation, without constraint of any kind. Conversely, the Plotinian universe is a great continuum or "chain of being" which proceeds downward from a supreme principle of goodness and power to the non-being of matter. The difference between lesser levels of reality or hypostases lies in the degree of their distance or separation from the One. For Augustine, on the other hand, creatures are wholly distinct from their creative cause.

As a Christian, Augustine viewed the world as fundamentally good, albeit imperfect, radically contingent and riddled with non-being. For Plotinus, the stumbling block was the very fact of otherness: *why* must anything other than the One exist? The paradox lies in the fact that the will to be other than the One is implicit in the One's very emanation. For Augustine, however, the stumbling block is not creation, but the fact of evil: how can evil manifest itself in a universe created by a supremely perfect God? In Augustinian terms, evil proceeds not from creation *per se*, but from a perversion of the will and the goods which God has created. By means of the "evil will" (*mala voluntas*), the soul turns from God and directs itself toward the possession of lesser goods. The chief expression of this "evil will" is pride (*superbia*).

In spite of the marked differences between the Plotinian and Augustinian visions of reality, *tolma* could have provided Augustine with a suitable referent for *superbia* from a number of standpoints. As demonstrated above, both terms designate "root faults" which precipitate the origin of evil within their respective approaches. But a number of other striking parallels between *tolma* and *superbia* emerge which further strengthen the hypothesis supporting an Augustinian "dependence" upon the *Enneads* for a philosophical understanding of the prime motive for the soul's aversion from God.

Superbia as Apostasy

In various places, Augustine characterizes the soul's fall as an apostasy, that is, a "standing away" from God which amounts to a rebellion against Divine authority. The proud soul's aversion is explicitly defined as an *apostatare a Deo*.[10] This phrase might be interpreted in two ways, each of which displays a Plotinian dimension. First, it can be interpreted as a bold, dynamic act whereby the soul separates itself from its Creator. Plotinus interpreted the willful movements of both Nous and Soul in such terms: *Ennead* VI.9(9).5.24-29 describes Nous as "daring" to stand apart from the One. Similarly, *Ennead* V.1(10).1.1-10 attributes the soul's error to a "standing apart" or separation from the father at a great distance. Secondly, *apostatare a Deo* might refer to a condition of estrangement which is tantamount to rebellion against a higher ontological principle: *Ennead* IV.2(1).(21).1.9-10 designates differentiation itself as an apostasy; *Ennead* V.1(10).5.1-2 attributes an intentional apostasy to souls, asserting that they wish to stand apart and exist on their own.

In the *De Genesi contra Manichaeos*, Augustine explicitly links *superbia* with the *apostatare a Deo* theme: the beginning of pride, it relates, is man's apostasy from God (*initium enim superbia hominis apostatare a Deo*).[11] The phrase preserves the dual Plotinian connotation of (1) a willful movement from God, which amounts to (2) a subversion of Divine authority. Augustine proceeds from the teaching of *Ecclesiasticus* (10:9-14) as support for the thesis that pride initiates all sin. This key Scriptural text also provides the source of the "swelling" imagery which figures so prominently in Augustine's deliberations on the origins of iniquity: the soul "swelled" with pride, which is the beginning of sin (*intumescit superbia, quod est initium omnis peccati*).[12] *Superbia* constitutes a projection or expansion into the relative non-being of temporal existence. In this regard, Augustine uses another image with marked Plotinian overtones:

figuratively, the proud soul "spews forth" its innermost good (*per superbiam intima sua*).[13] Such an image calls to mind Plotinus's characterization of the distended Soul "uncoiling like a seed" in *Ennead* III.7(45).11.15-23.

The *De Musica* amplifies Augustine's characterization of *superbia* as an *apostatare a Deo*. As in the *De Genesi contra Manichaeos*, the soul's aversion from God is viewed in terms of an outward expansion of its interests and range of commitments: ". . . to puff with pride is to go forth to the outermost . . . giving up the inmost things (*intima projicere*), that is, putting yourself away from God . . ."[14] In the *De Musica*, Augustine discusses two implications of *superbia* and the soul's movement from God.

First, *superbia* precipitates the soul's commitment to what Augustine describes as "certain actions of its own power" (*superbia labi animam ad actiones quasdam potestatis sua*).[15] In this sense, *superbia* inspires a drive for autonomy similar to that initiated by *tolma* in Plotinus's scheme: according to Augustine, the proud soul wishes to exist for itself (*ad seipsam*) or through itself (*per seipsam*).[16] Augustine develops the same theme in both the *De moribus ecclesiae catholicae et de moribus Manichaeorum* (I,12), where he defines the soul's sin in terms of a desire for its own power (*suae potestatis esse cupit*) and in the *Soliloquia* (I,15), where he warns against an excessive reliance upon one's own powers to the exclusion of God (*noli ese velle quasi proprius et in tua potestate*). *Ennead* V.1(10).1.1-10 contains similar language, emphasizing that souls driven by *tolma* desire to be on their own. Such sentiments are also expressed in *Ennead* III.7(45).11.15-23, where the hypostasis Soul is said to desire self-determination, forfeiting its participation in the self-contained noetic world. In Augustine, the will for self-determination is an expression of the *superbia* which is the beginning of sin. The soul's desire to be its own master (*suae potestatis vult esse*) prompts a turning toward a good of its very own (*ad proprium convertitur*).[17]

The soul's option for a good proper to itself alone refers us to the second implication of *superbia* discussed in the *De Musica*: neglecting or disobeying universal law, the soul is committed to doing certain things private to itself (*universali lege neglecta in agenda quaedam cecidisse*).[18] Such "private" acts seem to coincide with the soul's association with bodily life. In the words of the *De Genesi contra Manichaeos*, the fallen soul is "condemned to the mortality of this life" (*in hujus vitae mortalitatem damnatus est*), bound to a corruptible body.[19] *Superbia* pits the soul against universal Divine law and confines it to a narrow sphere of interests. Drawing upon the insights of *Ennead* VI.4(22)-5(23)—in the Plotinian treatise "*On Omnipresence*"–Augustine relies upon the *commune/proprium* distinction which he fully develops in the *De libero arbitrio*: because the perfect Good is common to all, it cannot be the property or exclusive possession of anyone.[20] Through *superbia*, the soul opts for a good proper to itself alone, relinquishing its participation in a greater, all-encompassing Good.

Such a whole/part dichotomization can be further traced to *Ennead* IV.8(6).4.10-12, which describes the soul's descent from the universal to become partial and self-centered: in this context, the fallen soul is viewed as a "deserter" from the totality of things. Another Plotinian parallel is available: *Ennead* IV.7((2).13.4-15 describes the soul's descent in terms of an outward movement, an act whereby the soul chooses to administer the partial. In Plotinus, the conflict between a commitment to the totality of things and a focus upon a partial, circumscribed sphere is apparent on every level of the intelligible universe: in *Nous*, it manifests itself as a desire to be other than the One; in souls, it manifests itself in the desire to abandon the administration of the cosmos in favor of the supervision of a particular body. Augustine retains the spirit of these Plotinian insights: by virtue of its proud *lapsus*, the soul commits acts "private" to itself, that is, acts proper to a soul that is unduly absorbed in the life of the senses. As a result, it subjects itself to all of the vicissitudes enumerated in the *De Genesi contra Manichaeos*: a difficulty in finding Truth, torment by nettling doubts and questions, perplexity, a burdening with daily cares, and the struggle for daily sustenance.[21]

Superbia as Idolatry

In addition to his characterization of *superbia* as an *apostatare a Deo*, Augustine also describes this primal sin in a manner which calls to mind the Scriptural sin of idolatry. The *De Genesi contra Manichaeos* condemns the proud who "allocate to themselves that which is not proper to them" (*qui sibi arrogantes quod non*).[22] In the *De Genesi contra Manichaeos*, Augustine further defines *superbia* as a refusal to submit oneself to Divine authority, or, to exist "under God" (*sub Deo*).[23] The proud soul wishes to be like God, or more drastically, God's equal (*cum Deo esse pares vellent*), turning from Truth to itself (*ab ea ergo veritate quisquis aversus est, et ad seipsam conversus*).[24] The *De moribus ecclesiae catholicae et de moribus Manichaeorum* articulates a similar teaching: Augustine asserts that audacity (*audacia*) prompts the soul to desire to be God-like (*audacia qua vult esse similior*), that is, to be its own master as God is (*sua potestatis esse cupit ut Deus est*).[25] In effect, *superbia* or *audacia* motivate the soul to claim the Divine prerogative as its own.

As used in this context, both *superbia* and *audacia* exhibit some interesting parallels with Plotinian *tolma*. The ambiguity of meaning that we have observed in *tolma* permits it to be interpreted not only as a rebellious pride, but also an audacious daring or venturesomeness to embark upon an independent course of action. In the *Enneads*, souls are said to descend in response to an urge to actualize their own potentialities to supervise and to govern individual bodies. In effect, they engage in a kind of "imitative creation" by acting on their own and exercising a direct, "hands on" involvement with the bodies they animate. A narcissistic element appears to be present in such activity. In a sense, the soul becomes "enamoured" of its own creative potential and power for self-assertion. *Ennead* IV.4(28).3 presents a closely related argument, attributing the motive for souls' descent to a self-love which prompts them to exist on their own. [26]

In several works, Augustine interprets the soul's sin in terms of a desire to imitate Divine power or omnipotence. In the *De Musica*, he asserts that the proud soul prefers to imitate God rather than to serve Him (*quo vitio Deum imitari, quam Deo servire anima maluit*).[27] The *De Vera Religione* likewise defines *superbia* as a "perverse imitation of Divine omnipotence" (*perversa scilicet imitatione omnipotentis dei*).[28] Such an aspiration to Divine power constitutes, in the words of the *Confessiones*, a futile exercise in "deformed liberty" (*manca libertas*)–a willful drive toward nothingness that parallels the tolmatic surge toward non-being in the *Enneads*.[29] What better illustrates this destructive movement than the "theft of pears" episode in the *Confessiones* ? As Augustine states, no good was sought in the boys' theft and vandalism; the deed was wholly irrational, serving no useful purpose at all. Yet, Augustine and his companions relish their fleeting sense of power and the exhilaration derived from self-assertion, wantonness, and brute force.

For Augustine, freedom is deformed when the soul loves itself or material goods above God. Augustine relies upon a Stoic insight which is operative throughout his deliberations on human volition: the soul can never be free as long as it bases its happiness upon fleeting, transitory goods that can be involuntarily lost. The very transience and instability of such things mocks the will, because it can never fully possess them. True freedom and genuine power are not attained in the world, but only by submitting oneself to God, the eternal, changeless Good.[30]

The proud soul plunges into what the *De Vera Religione* characterizes as a "servitude to the desire of excelling" (*excellentiae*): in Augustinian terms, this constitutes one of the basest forms of idolatry, because it enslaves the soul to the pursuit of empty temporal triumphs and petty successes.[31] Like *curiositas and concupiscentia carnis, superbia* represents a distorted love or perversion of the will which makes inferior things the objects of the soul's desire.[32] The proud soul "swells" outward (*cum superbia vel tumore*), seeking to aggrandize itself by dominating other souls and lesser creatures.[33] In this sense, it violates the "rule of perfect religion" alluded to above (*De Vera Religione* 10,19): failing to acknowledge its contingency before God, it serves the creature instead of the Creator.

Action *versus* Contemplation

The proud soul's desire to imitate Divine power is intimately related to another key Augustinian theme: *superbia* is also characterized as the "general love of action" (*generalis vero amor actionis*).[34] *Superbia* and *tolma* are, in fact, both connected with the initiation of action, movement, and temporal process. Both terms give rise to a spirit of inquietude which stands in opposition to a contemplative mode of existence. *Enneads* V.1(10).1.1-10 and III.7(45).11.15-23 provide key Plotinian referents.

According to *Ennead* V.1(10).1.1-10, souls driven by *tolma* tend toward temporal process, delight in their freedom of self-determination, and make great use of their self-movement. The *De Genesi contra Manichaeos* provides an interesting parallel to these sentiments: in Augustinian terms, the proud soul exults in the "quasi-freedom" of its own movement (*de suis motibus quasi liberis exsultat*).[35] In both Plotinus and Augustine, the soul's exhilaration is deceptive, since its supposed freedom results in a severe impairment and limitation of its power.

Ennead III.7(45).11.15-23 likewise discusses the dynamics of this surge toward freedom of movement in the context of Soul's temporalization. As we have seen, Plotinus likened this expansive movement to the uncoiling or dispersion of the powers of a seed. In *Ecclesiasticus* (10:9-14), Augustine found an image similar to that of the uncoiling seed. In that Scriptural passage, the proud man "spews forth" his innermost good (*projecit intima sua*). In this respect, the language of the *Confessiones* provides an excellent synthesis of Plotinian and Scriptural insights in its comprehensive definition of iniquity:

> I asked 'What is iniquity?' and I found that it is not a substance. it is perversity of will, twisted away from the supreme substance, yourself, O God, and towards lower things, and casting away its innermost self and swelling beyond itself (*sed a summa substantia, te Deo detortae in infima voluntatis perversitatem, projicientis intima sua, et tumescentis foras*). [36]

By means of the imagery derived from *Ennead* III.7(45).11.15-23 and *Ecclesiasticus* (10:9-14), Augustine was able to link *superbia* directly with the soul's gravitation toward the temporal manifold. *Superbia* turns the soul away from God, the fullness of being and source of eternal Truth, and directs it toward the *vanitas* or groundlessness of temporal things. The early *De Ordine* discusses the "emptiness" (*inanescere*) which accompanies *superbia*: the proud soul subjects itself to an ontological privation or "mental beggary" which involves it in a futile striving after unstable phantasms.[37] Again, the *Confessiones* provides an effective image: Augustine describes his own sinful condition in disparaging terms as a "land of want" (*regio egestatis*).[38] He might have employed such paradoxical terminology as a means of translating similar Plotinian paradoxes: the *Enneads* refer to the "poverty" or deficiency of formless matter (*Ennead* III.6(26).14.10-18); likewise, Plotinus depicts Soul's temporalization in terms of an overextension or negative expansion of its faculties to a "weaker greatness" (*Ennead* III.7(45).11.26-27).

The general term which Augustine used to describe the soul's gravitation toward temporality is *excurrere*, that is, a "running over and downwards." *Excurrere* finds an excellent Plotinian parallel in the verb *exillo* , which Plotinus used to describe the dispersion of Soul when it "uncoils" itself like a seed (*Ennead* III.7(45).11.24). Both *excurrere* and *exillo* designate an outward expansion or excursion into non-being. But in addition to *excurrere*, one might also add *defluere, defluxus*, and *distentio* as possible Augustinian translations of Plotinianisms which express the downward movement of being into a life of temporal involvement and spiritual turmoil.

Augustine's "Creative Adaptation" of Plotinus

The foregoing considerations demonstrate some rather marked affinities between Plotinian *tolma* and *superbia*, the root of Augustine's moral triad. In the *Enneads*, Augustine could have easily found a philosophical source which reinforced his belief in the Scriptural dictum that pride (*superbia*) is the beginning of all sin (*Ecclesiasticus* 10:9-14). The kinship between *tolma* and *superbia* is reflected in the various parallels which emerge when one compares the roles of these terms. First, *tolma* and *superbia* represent "root faults" in Plotinus and Augustine, respectively. Secondly, *tolma* and *superbia* are closely associated with a spirit of apostasy, or more precisely, a "standing-apart" from a higher ontological principle. Third, *tolma* and *superbia* are closely connected with the theme of idolatry: in a Plotinian context, the "idolatry" of *tolma* lies in the soul's desire to be on its own, in its desire to engage in an imitative creation by supervising an individual body, and in overextending its powers; in an Augustinian context, idolatry coincides with a refusal to exist under God. Augustine further roots this idolatrous desire to be God-like in *audacia*, a term extremely close to *tolma* in its connotations of assertiveness, boldness, and venturesomeness. The final indication of a kinship between *tolma* and *superbia* lies in the mutual connection of these terms with action, movement, and temporal involvement.

But while such parallels can be established, one must be equally sensitive to the differences between the philosophies of Plotinus and Augustine. These differences bring to the fore a question regarding Augustine's so-called "dependence" upon the *Enneads*: to what extent could Augustine apply Plotinian insights to the interpretation of Christian teaching? Augustine did not merely rely upon the *Enneads* in a passive manner and mechanically transfer its insights to his own system of thought. Rather, he was required to perform some delicate conceptual "grafting," involving both the introduction of Plotinian ideas into his own tradition, and a reshaping and adapting of these ideas to suit his own philosophical and theological purposes. But the success of any grafting procedure demands an ability to assimilate some new, and perhaps, alien element. But in assimilating the new element, the host transforms and subsumes it. A synthesis of two dissimilar elements is thereby achieved. As a Christian philosopher, Augustine undertook such a procedure, selectively implanting Plotinian ideas into his Judeo-Christian world-view. His discussions of *superbia* thus exhibit a skillful interweaving and reciprocal recasting of Plotinian and Scriptural themes. In philosophical terms, Augustine's sense of detachment from what he perceived as the emptiness of worldly affairs could readily find an outlet in the otherworldly dimension of the *Enneads*.

The distrust of the sense world and the devaluation of the body that we find in the *Enneads* seem to have held a special attraction for the recent convert from Manichaeism. For the man who embraced Christianity in 386 A.D. was the same individual who had embraced the radical dualism of the Manichaeans about a decade earlier, and subsequently, Plotinian Neoplatonism. The Christian Augustine affirmed the inherent goodness of the whole of creation. Yet, he continued to approach the world of sense experience through the eyes of the Neoplatonist, with all of the distrust and suspicion toward the realm of becoming inherent in that tradition. This attitude was complemented by the Stoic ideal of indifference to a world of instability and change. Such influences were to shape his metaphysical, epistemological, and moral approaches in a decisive manner.

Notes

1. The greater part of this discussion originally appeared under the title "St. Augustine's Treatment of *superbia* and its Plotinian Affinities" in *Augustinian Studies* XVIII (1987):66-80.

2. The renewed interest in this topic is an outgrowth of work begun in the nineteenth century. For early works which attempted to establish Plotinian parallels in the Augustinian corpus, see: M. N. Bouilet, *Les Ennéades de Plotin*, 3 volumes (Paris, 1857-1861); L. Grandgeorge, *Saint Augustin et le Neoplatonisme* (Paris, 1896); Prosper Alfaric, *L'Evolution Intellectualle de Saint Augustin* (Paris,1918); Charles Boyer, *Christianisme et néoplatonisme dans la formation de Saint Augustin* (Rome, 1923); Jens Nörregaard, *Augustins Bekehrung* (Tubingen, 1923).

3. Various publications by O'Connell provide sufficient, compelling evidence for accepting this as a plausible hypothesis. The following list includes references to O'Connell's publications, along with major criticisms of his thesis: R. J. O'Connell, *"Ennead VI, 4-5 in the Work of St. Augustine,"* *Revue des Etudes Augustiniennes* (1963): 1-39; "The Plotinian Fall of the Soul in St. Augustine," *Traditio* 19(1963): 1-35; "The *Enneads* And St. Augustine's Image of Happiness," *Vigiliae Christianae* 17 (1963): 129-164; "The Riddle of St. Augustine's Confessions: A Plotinian Key," *International Philosophical Quarterly* 4 (1964): 327-372; Goulven Madec, a note in *Revue des Études Augustiniennes* 11 (1965): 372-375; Olivier DuRoy, *L'Intelligence de la Foi en la Trinité selon Saint Augustin* (Paris, 1966); R. J. O'Connell, *St. Augustine's Early Theory of Man*, A.D. 386-391 (Cambridge, Mass.: Harvard University Press, 1968); Goulven Madec, "Une lecture de Confessions VII, ix, 13-xxi, 27," *Revue des Études Augustiniennes* 16 (1970): 79-137; F. E. VanFleteren, O.S.A., "Authority and Reason, Faith and Understanding in the Thought of St. Augustine, *Augustinian Studies* 4 (1973): 33-72; G. J. P. O'Daly, "Did St. Augustine Ever Believe in the Soul's Pre-Existence?" *Augustinian Studies* 5 (1974): 227-235; R. J. O'Connell, "Pre-Existence in the Early Augustine," *Revue des Études Augustiniennes* 26 (1980): 176-188; "Faith, Reason, and Ascent to Vision in St. Augustine," *Augustinian Studies* 11 (1980). A number of works attempt to establish that Plotinus's disciple Porphyry provided the Neoplatonic inspiration for Augustine's writings. In this regard, see W. Theiler, *Porphyrios und Augustin* (Halle, 1933). Theiler's thesis was undermined soon after its publication by Paul Henry in *Plotin et l'Occident* (Louvain, 1934). J. J. O'Meara provides another attempt to

support a Porphyrian rather than a Plotinian influence in his Porphyry's *Philosophy From Oracles in Augustine* (Paris, 1959). In this vein, also see F. E. VanFleteren, "Authority and Reason, Faith and Understanding in the Thought of St. Augustine," *Augustinian Studies* 4 (1973): 33-72 and R. J. O'Connell's response, "Faith and Reason, and Ascent to Vision in St. Augustine," *Augustinian Studies* 11 (1980).

4. R.J. O'Connell, S.J., *St. Augustine's Early Theory of Man*, A.D. 386-391 (Cambridge, Mass.: Harvard University Press, 1968), pp. 173-83. This hypothesis grows out of a larger one which maintains that the *Enneads* provided Augustine with the intellectual matrix within which he attained a philosophical understanding of Christian teaching.

cf. The affinities between *tolma* and at least *superbia* has been recognized by Olivier DuRoy (*L'Intelligence de la Foi en la Trinité selon Saint Augustin* (Paris, 1966), p. 345,n.2) supports O'Connell's thesis on this particular point: "Je suis entièrement d'accord avec lui voir dans Enn. V,I,1,1-8. un texte bien connu d'Augustin comme l'avait déjà montré A. Solignac. De même la composante plotinienne (*tolma*) de la superbia augustinienne est indubitable comme on le voit dans le *De Mor.*,I,12,20,PL,XXXII,1320, où Augustin l'appelle *audacia* et en definit l'intention *par suae potestatis esse cupiti*."

5. The *De Beata Vita* (I,3) cites the "proud eagerness of vain glory" (*superbium studium inanimisse*) as the greatest obstacle to happiness; the *Contra Academicos* (II,18) characterizes pride as the "most loathsome vice" (*in superbiae, quo vitio nihil est immanius*); the *De Quantitate Animae* (34,78) describes the "deceptive desire of vain glory" (*inanis gloriae cupiditate decepti*) as the means whereby we plunge from the heights and sink to the lowest depths.

6. *De Genesi contra Manichaeos* II,9(12); *De Musica* VI,13(40).

7. *De Genesi contra Manichaeos* II,9(12); *De Musica* VI,13(40).

8. *De Vera Religione* 10(19).

9. *De Genesi contra Manichaeos* II,9(12); *De Musica* VI,13(40).

10. *De Genesi contra Manichaeos* II,5(6); *De Musica* VI,6(53).

11. *De Genesi contra Manichaeos* II,5(6).

12. *De Genesi contra Manichaeos* II,9(12).

13. *De Genesi contra Manichaeos* II,9(12).

14. *De Musica* VI,13(40). Translated by R.C. Taliaferro, *Fathers of the Church* (Washington, D.C.: Catholic University of America Press, 1947).

15. *De Musica* VI,16(53). Taliaferro translation.

16. *De Musica* VI,13(40); VI,16(53); *De Genesi contra Manichaeos* II,9(12).

17. *De libero arbitrio* II,19(53).

18. *De Musica* VI,16(53).

19. *De Genesi contra Manichaeos* I,18(29).

20. *De libero arbitrio* II,7ff. See R.J. O'Connell, S.J., *St. Augustine's Early Theory of Man* . . . (cf. note 1, above), pp. 31-64, for an analysis of Augustine's absorption and adaptation of Plotinus's theory of Omnipresence.

21. *De Genesi contra Manichaeos* II,20(30).

22. *De Genesi contra Manichaeos* II,26(40).

23. *De Genesi contra Manichaeos* II,15(22).

24. *De Genesi contra Manichaeos* II,15(22).

25. *De moribus ecclesiae catholicae et de moribus Manichaeorum* I,12(20).

26. cf. *Enneads* IV.8(6).2 and IV.3(27).12 (the passage containing the "mirror of Dionysius" allegory).

27. *De Musica* VI,13(40).

28. *De Vera Religione* 45(84).

29. *Confessiones* II,6 (trans. J.K. Ryan, Garden City, New York: Image Books, 1960).

30. *De Vera Religione* 45(84).

31. *De Vera Religione* 38(69).

32. *De libero arbitrio* II,14(37).

33. *De Vera Religione* 38(69).

34. *De Musica* VI,13(40).

35. *De Genesi contra Manichaeos* II,16(24).

36. *Confessiones* VII,16(22). Ryan translation.

37. *De Ordine* I,2(3).

38. *Confessiones* II,10(18).

Bibliography

Aristotle. *The Basic Works*. Edited with an introduction by Richard McKeon. New York: Random House, 1941.

Armstrong, A. H. "Form, Individual and Person in Plotinus," *Dionysius* (1977): 49-68.

_____. "Gnosis and Greek Philosophy," *Gnosis. Festschrift für Hans Jonas*. Göttingen: Vandenhoeck and Ruprecht, 1978.

_____. "Spiritual or Intelligible Matter in Plotinus and St. Augustine," *Augustinus Magister I*. Paris, 1965.

_____. *The Architecture of the Intelligible Universe in the Philosophy of Plotinus*. Cambridge: Cambridge University Press, 1940.

_____. *The Cambridge History of Later Greek and Early Medieval Philosophy*. Cambridge: Cambridge University Press, 1970.

St. Augustine of Hippo. *Patrologiae Cursus Completus Augustini Opera Omnia*. Edited by J. P. Migne (Paris, 1841, ff.).

_____. *Corpus Christianorum. Series Latina. Aurelii Augustini Opera*. Turnholti: Typographi Brepols Editores Pontificii, 1962, ff.).

_____. *Oeuvres de Saint Augustin*. Volumes 4, 5, 6, 7, 8. Paris: Desclee De Brouwer, 1976.

_____. *Fathers of the Church*. Washington, D.C.: Catholic University of America Press, 1947, ff.

_____. *Confessions*. Translated by John K. Ryan. Garden City, New York: Image Books, 1960.

Baladi, Naguib. *La Penseé de Plotin*. Paris: Presses Universitaires de France, 1970.

____. "Origine et Signification de l'Audace chez Plotin," *Le Néoplatonisme*. Paris, 1971.

Blumenthal, Henry. "Did Plotinus Believe in Ideas of Individuals?" *Phronesis* 11 (1966): 62-80.

____. "Nous and Soul in Plotinus." *Plotino e il Neoplatonismo* (1974): 203-219.

____. "Soul, World-Soul and Individual Soul in Plotinus," *Le Néoplatonisme*. Paris, 1971.

Bréhier, Emile. *The Philosophy of Plotinus*. Translated by Joseph Thomas. Chicago: The University of Chicago Press, 1971.

Cornford, F. M. "Mysticism and Science in the Pythagorean Tradition," *The Classical Quarterly* XVII (1923): 1-12.

Copleston, F. C., S. J. *A History of Philosophy*. 20 Volumes. Garden City, New York: Image Books, 1962.

Costello, Edward B. "Is Plotinus Inconsistent on the Nature of Evil?" *International Philosophical Quarterly* 7 (1961): 483-497.

DeVogel, C. J. *Greek Philosophy. A Collection of Texts with Notes and Translations*. 3 Volumes. Leiden: E. J. Brill, 1953.

____. "On the Neoplatonic Character of Platonism and the Platonic Character of Neoplatonism," *Mind* 62 (1953): 43-64.

Dill, Samuel. *Roman Society from Nero to Marcus Aurelius*. London: Macmillan, 1920.

Dillon, John. "The Descent of the Soul in Middle Platonism and Gnostic Theory," *The Rediscovery of Gnosticism*. Volume I. Leiden: E. J. Brill, 1980.

____. *The Middle Platonists*. London: Duckworth & Co., Ltd., 1977.

Dodds, E. R. "Numenius and Ammonius," *Les Sources de Plotin*: 1-32. Foundation Hardt: Vandoeuvres-Geneve, 1960.

_____. Editor. *Journal and Letters of Stephen MacKenna.* New York: William Morrow and Company, 1937.

_____. *Pagan and Christian in an Age of Anxiety.* Cambridge: Cambridge University Press, 1968.

_____. *The Greeks and the Irrational.* Berkeley and Los Angeles: The University of California Press, 1973.

_____. "The Parmenides of Plato and the Origin of the Neoplatonic One," *Classical Quarterly* 22 (1928): 129-142.

_____. "Tradition and Personal Achievement in the Philosophy of Plotinus," *The Ancient Concept of Progress.* Oxford: Oxford University Press, 1973.

Festugiere, A. J. *La Revelation d'Hermes Trismegiste* III. Paris, 1953.

Glare, G. W. Editor. *Oxford Latin Dictionary.* Oxford: Clarendon Press, 1982.

Greene, William Chase. *Moira: Fate, Good, and Evil in Greek Thought.* Cambridge, Mass.: Harvard University Press, 1944.

Guthrie, W. C. K. *The Greek Philosophers from Thales to Aristotle.* New York: Harper Colophon, 1975.

Henry, Paul. *Plotin et l'Occident.* Louvain, 1934.

_____. "The Place of Plotinus in the History of Thought." Introductory Essay in Stephen MacKenna's translation of the *Enneads* of Plotinus. New York: Pantheon Books. London: Faber and Faber, 1969.

Inge, W. R. *Mysticism in Religion.* London: Rider and Co., 1969.

_____. *The Philosophy of Plotinus.* The Gifford Lectures, 1917-1918. London: Longmans, Green and Co., 1923.

Irenaeus. *The Writings of Irenaeus*. Translated by Roberts-Rambaut. Edinburgh, 1884.

James, William. "The Will to Believe." *Classical and Contemporary Readings in the Philosophy of Religion*. Second Edition. Edited by John Hick. Englewood Cliffs, New Jersey: Prentice-Hall, 1970.

Jaspers, Karl. *Way to Wisdom*. Translated by Ralph Manheim. New Haven: Yale University Press, 1962.

Jonas, Hans. *The Gnostic Problem*. Boston: Beacon Press, 1963.

____. "The Soul in Gnosticism and Plotinus," *Le Néoplatonisme*. Paris, 1971.

Katz, Joseph. "Plotinus and the Gnostics," *Journal of the History of Ideas* XV (1954): 289-298.

Liddell and Scott. *Greek-English Lexicon*. Oxford: Oxford University Press, 1953.

MacRae, G. W. "Hermetic Literature." *New Catholic Encyclopedia* VI (1967 Edition): 1076-1077.

Mamo, P. S. "Forms of Individuals in the *Enneads*," *Phronesis* XIV (1969): 77-96.

Merlan, Philip. *From Platonism to Neoplatonism*. The Hague: Martinus Nijhoff, 1960.

____. *Monopsychism, Mysticism, Metaconsciousness*. The Hague: Martinus Nijhoff, 1963.

The Nag Hammadi Codices. Facsimiles, Translations, Commentaries, Studies. (Leiden: E. J. Brill, 1971, ff.).

The Nag Hammadi Library in English. Directed by J. M. Robinson and translated by members of the Coptic Gnostic Library Project of the Institute for Antiquity and Christianity. Leiden: E. J. Brill, 1977.

Numenius. *The Neoplatonic Writings of Numenius.* Collected and Translated by Kenneth Guthrie. Laurence, Kansas: Selene Books, 1987.

O'Brien, D. B. "Plotinus on Evil," *Downside Review* LXXXVII (1969): 68-112.

O'Daly, G. J. P. "Did St. Augustine Ever Believe in the Soul's Pre-Existence?" *Augustinian Studies* 5 (1974): 227-235.

Origen. *On First Principles (De Principiis).* Translated by G. W. Butterworth. New York: Harper Torchbooks, 1966.

Pearson, Birger A. "The Tractate *Marsanes* (NHC X) and the Platonic Tradition," *Gnosis.* A Festschrift für Hans Jonas. Göttingen: Vandenhoeck and Ruprecht, 1978.

Plato. *The Collected Dialogues of Plato.* Edited with an introduction and prefatory notes by Edith Hamilton and Huntington Cairns. Translated by Lane Cooper and others. New York: Pantheon Books, 1961.

Plotinus. *A Volume of Selections.* Translated by A. H. Armstrong. London: Allen & Unwin, Ltd., 1953.

_____. Translated by A. H. Armstrong. 7 Volumes. Loeb Classical Library Edition. London: William Heinemann Ltd. and Cambridge, Mass.: Harvard University Press, 1966-1984.

_____. Plotinus: *Ennead V.1 On the Three Principal Hypostases.* A Commentary with translation by Michael Atkinson. Oxford: Oxford University Press, 1983.

_____. *Ennéades.* Translated by Emile Bréhier. 7 Volumes. Paris: Societe D'Edition 'Les Belles Lettres,' 1924-1938.

_____. *Les Ennéades de Plotin.* Translated by M. N. Bouillet. 3 Volumes. Paris: 1857-1861.

_____. *The Enneads.* Translated by Stephen MacKenna. Revised by B. S. Page with an introduction by Paul Henry,

S. J. Fourth Edition. New York: Pantheon Books, Inc., 1969 and London: Faber and Faber, 1969.

_____. *Plotini Opera*. Edited by Paul Henry and Hans-Rudolf Schwyzer. Museum Lessianum Series Philosophica XXXIII, XXXIV, XXXV. Tomus I and II (Paris: Desclee De Brouwer; Bruxelles: L'Edition Universell, S. A., 1951, 1959). Tomus III (Bruxelles: Desclee De Brouwer; Leiden: E. J. Brill, 1973).

Puech, H. C. "Plotin et les Gnostiques," *Les Sources de Plotin*: 159-174 (and discussion, pp. 175-190). Foundation Hardt: Vandoeuvre-Geneve, 1960.

Rist, J. M. "Forms of Individuals in Plotinus," *Classical Quarterly* N. S. 13 (1963): 224-231.

_____. "Monism: Plotinus and Some Predecessors," *Harvard Studies in Classical Philology* 69 (1965): 329-344.

_____. Plotinus. *The Road to Reality*. Cambridge: Cambridge University Press, 1967.

_____. "The Indefinite Dyad and Intelligible Matter in Plotinus," *Classical Quarterly* N. S. 12 (1962): 99-107.

Runia, David T. Editor. *Plotinus Amid Gnostics and Christians*. Papers presented at the Plotinus Symposium held at the Free University, Amsterdam on 25 January 1984. Amsterdam: VU Uitgeverij/Free University Press, 1984.

Schwyzer, H. R. "Plotinus," *Real-Encyclopaedie der Klassischen Altertumwissenschaft*. Pauly-Wissowa-Kroll-Witter. Stuttgard, 1894, ff. XXI, Cols. 547-548.

Seligman, Paul. *Being and Non-Being*. The Hague: Martinus Nijhoff, 1974.

Stead, G. C. "The Valentinian Myth of Sophia," *The Journal of Theological Studies* N. S. 20 (1969): 75-104.

Torchia, N. Joseph. "Plotinian *Tolma* and the Fall of the Soul in the Early Philosophy of Saint Augustine," *Dissertation*

Abstracts International 48, No. 4 (1987), 941A (Fordham University).

____. "St. Augustine's Treatment of *superbia* and its Plotinian Affinities," Augustinian Studies XVIII (1987): 66-80.

____. "Satiety and the Fall of Souls in Origen's *De Principiis*," *Studia Patristica* XVIII-3: 455-462.

Wallis, R. T. *Neoplatonism*. New York: Charles Scribner's Sons, 1972.

Wilson, R. Mcl. *The Gnostic Problem*. London: A. R. Mowbray and Co., Ltd., 1958.

Zaehner, R. C. *Mysticism Sacred and Profane*. Oxford: Oxford University Press, 1980.

Zandee, J. *The Terminology of Plotinus and of some Gnostic Writings, mainly the Fourth Treatise of the Jung Codex.* Istanbul, 1961.

Indices

Index Locorum

General Index